According to the author the
must pay in order to move
yearning for greatness is ofte
hence Reno Johnson, has in
eral revelations about God's perfect plan and will for
our lives. This book is comprehensive in scope yet it is
written in a manner that makes it relevant to people
from many different walks of life. An extraordinary
book!

—Dr. Milton C. Woods
Bethel Deliverance Tabernacle International
Detroit, Michigan

Apostle Reno Johnson has an ardent passion that
drives him to pursue the power of God, which
enables him to accomplish his God-given assignments
and vision. The price for God's power and presence
in his life has been clearly demonstrated by his sac-
rifices and steadfast commitment. An apostolic and
prophetic voice to the nations, who releases revelatory
truth to the Body of Christ, I am delighted to recom-
mend this book as an invaluable tool that will equip
you for your next level in your walk with God.

—Apostle Ed Watson
Senior Pastor, Trinity "City of Praise"
Kingdom Covenant Connection,
Lead Apostle
Nassau, Bahamas

Many persons marvel at the glamour, power, and
fame that come with the anointing. However, this
timeless treasure can be very costly. Apostle Johnson
in *Paying the Price* helps the reader to identify the
purpose of his or her pain and unexpected encounters and drives them to push through in order to get
to the place of destiny. This book is a must read as it

has the potential to change lives and revitalize passion for excellence.

—Dr. Yvonne Capehart
Sister's Keepers Int'l Ministries/Yvonne
Capehart Ministries Int'l
Pensacola, Florida

Without question, Apostle Reno Johnson is a twenty-first century kingdom mantel revivalist and reformer. As an anointed biblical teacher he masterfully articulates insightful truths that are biblically sound and spiritually relevant to our times. Truly he is one who has his ear tuned to the very voice of God. This book is sure to shift you into a new dimension of God's kingdom!

—Apostle A. L. Albury
Senior Pastor, Kingdom Encounter Ministries,
International
Grand Bahama Island, Bahamas

Paying the Price is a masterful interpretation of the necessity of trials and tests that inevitably we all must endure. Apostle Reno Johnson has been used by the Lord to equip and empower you for life through this riveting and insightful revelation. Each chapter is filled with the principles of Scripture to produce victorious strategies in your life; truly a must read.

—Pastor Bruce C. Davis
President and founder, New Birth Church
International
Nassau, Bahamas

The purpose of life is most often fulfilled in our God given assignment for every season we live to encounter. Without a doubt God has given Apostle Johnson kingdom principles in accessing the passageway to positions of favor. His insight on the cost

for the anointing has enlightened the minds of those who are endeavoring to pursue that final place in God. The passage in paying the price quotes a key point from an old African proverb that says, "Smooth seas do not make skillful sailors." Likewise smooth times do not make skillful warriors; rather it is the rough times of life that does the molding and shaping. This is a must read.

—REVEREND TERRELL TURNER
CHIEF APOSTLE, WORD IN MOTION MINISTRIES
ATLANTA, GEORGIA

Paying the Price is another masterpiece penned by Apostle Johnson, who so competently maps out the journey one would have to take in order to arrive to a greater level of power and anointing in the kingdom. This book encourages its readers to pursue all that God has predetermined for them. Truly this book will be one of the many that will shift your life.

—GLENVILLE A. DAVIS, MBA
BANKER/COLLEGE PROFESSOR
NASSAU, BAHAMAS

PAYING THE PRICE

PAYING
THE
PRICE

DESTINED FOR GREATNESS:
ARE YOU WILLING TO PAY THE PRICE?

RENO I. JOHNSON

Paying the Price by Reno Johnson
Published by Creation House
A Charisma Media Company
600 Rinehart Road
Lake Mary, Florida 32746
www.charismamedia.com

Unless otherwise noted, all Scripture quotations are from the King James Version of the Bible.

Scripture quotations marked NKJV are from the New King James Version of the Bible. Copyright © 1979, 1980, 1982 by Thomas Nelson, Inc., Publishers. Used by permission.

Unless otherwise noted, English definitions are derived from Merriam-Webster Collegiate Dictionary.

Greek and Hebrew definitions are derived from *Strong's Exhaustive Concordance of the Bible*, ed. James Strong, Nashville, TN: Thomas Nelson Publishers, 1997.

Design Director: Bill Johnson
Cover design by Terry Clifton

Visit the author's website: www.ARJM.org, and www.DEMISITE.org.

Library of Congress Cataloging-in-Publication Data:
2012940598
International Standard Book Number: 978-1-62136-073-5

E-book International Standard Book Number:
978-1-62136-074-2

First edition

13 14 15 16 17 — 987654321

Printed in Canada

ACKNOWLEDGMENTS

WHILE SOME MAY view the anointing on your life as common, I imagine you paid a significant price to get to the place where you are spiritually. The anointing upon an individual varies according to the things he or she has suffered and the price they have paid.

This book, as the title suggests, seeks to make the reader aware of the cost associated with being anointed, called by God, and exercising the authority that comes from being a yielded vessel. Throughout the pages of this revelatory book the reader will find genuine accounts of actual experiences, receive sound advice and recommendations, and also discover the path to successfully being all that God has predetermined for you to be.

The material and resources used to complete this book were derived through the generosity of many church leaders, civil and social activists, colleagues, families, and friends. These men and women have impacted my life in ways that they cannot imagine. The contributors are too many to mention, but among this cluster of awesome people is a small group I especially want to mention: Divine Encounter Ministries International (DEMI Family), the people whom I am privileged to shepherd; the leaders and congregants have been a pillar of strength to me. Truly my family, friends, and colleagues have gone over and beyond the call of duty.

My deepest thanks goes to my wife, Shandaly, and to our two daughters, Ranaé and Reishonda, who stood by my side and understood fully "the price" I paid to answer the call to ministry.

Finally, as this book goes to press, I wish to thank Creation House for the hard work that they have invested in the fulfillment of this vision.

To the only wise God be glory, dominion, and power!

—APOSTLE RENO I JOHNSON
DIVINE ENCOUNTER MINISTRIES INTERNATIONAL

CONTENTS

Introduction. xv

Chapter One: The Anointing 1

Chapter Two: The Vessel. 17

Chapter Three: Paying the Price 31

Chapter Four: Thirtyfold, Sixtyfold, and Hundredfold Anointing. 45

Chapter Five: The Aftereffect 71

Chapter Six: Greater Works. 93

Notes 101

About the Author. 103

Contact the Author 105

Ministry Resources 107

INTRODUCTION

EVERYTHING THAT YOU would ever desire in this world that has any kind of value to it will cost you a high price. Whether it is a house, car, yacht, jet, etc., you are hoping to obtain someday, it will cost a great price, especially if it's of top quality. Some of us have been fortunate to obtain such valuable possessions through inheritance, the generosity of others, or simply hard work. Whatever the case may be, how we achieve these prized possessions often determines the value that we place on them. In the spiritual arena, the greatest achievement is to operate in the hundredfold anointing of God. It is a precious commodity that can be very costly!

In today's society, a higher cost of something is often associated with a greater quality. Such differentiation in the price and quality is seen in the sale of automobiles. For instance, the cost of a Toyota Corolla is drastically different from that of a Mercedes-Benz. Definitely this difference has to do with manufacturing requirements, scarcity of parts, and imaging of the vehicle. As it is in the natural, so it is in the spiritual. A greater anointing often demands a greater price. According to Jesus, "For unto whomsoever much is given, of him shall be much required" (Luke 12:48). Those who are called to a greater anointing will pay a greater price; and at the end of the day, it will all be worth it.

Those who have been chosen for the greater and are willing to pay the price will be placed in the midst of great opposition, heated battles, nerve-wracking trials, and fiery furnaces lit by their atrocious and furious enemies. Are you still willing to pay the price? The psalmist said: "They that trust in the LORD shall be as mount Zion, which cannot be removed, but abideth forever" (Ps. 125:1). Those who will carry this anointing, because of its costliness, must put their trust and confidence in God. It is God who has begun the good work and He will see it through to its completion. Oftentimes it is not the stress of the achievement but simply our inability to endure and trust God to bring to pass that which He has promised. The apostle Paul put it best when he said, "Faithful is he that calleth you, who also will do it" (1 Thess. 5:24). Paul did not say God might do it, but God will do it. Are you willing to pay the price?

Chapter One

THE ANOINTING

THE ANOINTING DEFINED

THE WORD *ANOINTING* is a term that is commonly used/known in many religious forums. Although more popular in Old Testament literature—King James Bible translation notes the word is used twenty-five times in the Old Testament and only three times in the New Testament—it is still a very modern concept. Even though the notion of "anointing," "anointed," and "to anoint," has gained momentum in recent times, there has been, however, an abridgement of the definition of these terms from the previous biblical references. For instance, in keeping with Old Testament tradition, the "anointing" represented a type of consecration of items, places, or people set aside as holy for the service of God (see Exodus 29:29; 30:26; Leviticus 4:3). The word *anointing* derives from the word *anoint*; and according to Webster's dictionary, the word *anoint* means to rub or sprinkle on; to consecrate or make sacred in a ceremony, which includes applying oil and to dedicate to the service of God. "Anointing," as used in this chapter, makes inference to the applying of oil, anointment, or a similar substance as a sign of sanctification or consecration. In addition, anointing may also denote a medical remedy used

1

to heal miscellaneous illnesses. (See Isaiah 1:6; Mark 6:13; James 5:14.)

While the anointing—to rub or sprinkle on—of the sick and praying for their recovery is known as a Roman Catholic Church sacrament, it has its root in Christian doctrine. The Book of James boldly asserts: "Is anyone among you sick? Let him call for the elders of the church, and let them pray over him, anointing him with oil in the name of the Lord" (James 5:14, NKJV). Several accounts are given in the New Testament of dead bodies that have been anointed prior to burial (see Mark 14:8; Luke 23:56); and I believe in these end times, as the oil of God touches dead corpses, they will live again.

This is the season in which the power of God will once again be manifested through His vessels: the sick will be healed, the blind will receive their sight, the lame will walk, the dumb will talk, and even the dead will be raised to life. God is releasing a supernatural anointing upon His chosen vessels who will exercise unusual power. Thus, in a spiritual sense, the anointing is to have God (Jesus Christ, the Anointed One) poured on, smeared all over, and rubbed into humanity through His Spirit; this allows Him to operate in and through us in wisdom, power, and might. In essence, the anointing is God on flesh and working through flesh, doing only what God can do. There is a price, however, to be paid for this level of anointing. Are you willing to pay the price?

In this age where end-time prophecy is rapidly unfolding and the coming of Jesus Christ draws nigh, more folks are seeking to know and understand about the coming of the Messiah—the Anointed One—as predicted by Old Testament prophets (Daniel 9:25–26; Isaiah 61:1) and New Testament writings (John 1:41; Acts 9:22; 17:2–3; 18:5, 28).

Since Jesus is the Anointed One and we are joint heirs with Jesus Christ, we are designated to partake in the anointing. Hence, throughout this chapter the term *anointing* also refers to the supernatural divine enablement for God's chosen vessels to accomplish His (God's) will here on earth. God's work cannot be accomplished by human might nor power but only by His Spirit. Therefore the Bible declares in Zechariah 4:6b, "Not by might, nor by power, but by my spirit, saith the Lord of hosts." With this being said, we must realize that there is no power in the oil by itself but it is the Spirit of God that breathes into the oil to bring supernatural results—healing, deliverance, miracles, etc.—upon contact. A popular misconception is that the oil smeared on has the power to transform. You can pray and pour as much oil over yourself as you can find; but without the supernatural force of God, there will be no results—absolutely nothing will happen. The anointing of God brings life.

The invisible force behind the ministries of John Wesley, Smith Wigglesworth, Lester Sumrall, and Kathryn Kuhlman of the evangelical world is God's anointing. Gone are the days when man-made anointing will suffice; the men and women that God is raising up in this hour will function in a divine anointing.

This anointing, firstly, works in us by causing transformation to take place and by cultivating us to hear, understand, receive, and apply His Word, which will prepare us for ministry. This is what I call a preparatory anointing. I have been involved in ministry for over sixteen years; and during this time I have discovered that God sets an anointing upon His servants that enables them to serve Him fully at every level. There were times when an unusual anointing would rest upon me minutes before delivering a message from the mouth of God. As I matured in the things of God, I came to realize that God anoints an individual according to the unprecedented task that is assigned to them.

Secondly, the anointing works with us and through us by giving us the ability to do whatever God has called us to do: be it miracles of healing, casting out demons, prophesying, preaching, etc. The anointing qualifies, motivates, ignites, and energizes every servant of God for kingdom business. The price that you are willing to pay determines the level of anointing you will operate in. Are you willing to pay the price?

The anointing qualifies, motivates, ignites, and energizes every servant of God for kingdom business

---

The Holy Anointing Oil

While the anointing for the most part refers to a mysterious spiritual element, there is a tangible anointing oil that is explicitly described in the Book of Exodus. Here we find God giving Moses specific instructions on the components of the holy oil and its use in the anointing ceremonies.

> Moreover the Lord spake unto Moses, saying, Take thou also unto thee principal spices, of pure myrrh five hundred shekels, and of sweet cinnamon half so much, even two hundred and fifty shekels, and of sweet calamus two hundred and fifty shekels, And of cassia five hundred shekels, after the shekel of the sanctuary, and of oil olive an hin: And thou shalt make it an oil of holy ointment, an ointment compound after the art of the apothecary: it shall be an holy anointing oil. And thou shalt anoint the tabernacle of the

congregation therewith, and the ark of the testimony, And the table and all his vessels, and the candlestick and his vessels, and the altar of incense, And the altar of burnt offering with all his vessels, and the laver and his foot. And thou shalt sanctify them, that they may be most holy: whatsoever toucheth them shall be holy. And thou shalt anoint Aaron and his sons, and consecrate them, that they may minister unto me in the priest's office. And thou shalt speak unto the children of Israel, saying, This shall be an holy anointing oil unto me throughout your generations. Upon man's flesh shall it not be poured, neither shall ye make any other like it, after the composition of it: it is holy, and it shall be holy unto you. Whosoever compoundeth any like it, or whosoever putteth any of it upon a stranger, shall even be cut off from his people.

—Exodus 30:22–33

Moses received a complete manual of God's holy anointing oil—how it was to be made and used. It was to be used to anoint the tabernacle of the congregation, the ark of the testimony (covenant), the tables and all the vessels, the candlestick and the vessels, the altar of incense, the altar of burnt offering with all the vessels, and the laver and foot for the purpose of sanctification for holy service. Also, the anointing oil was for anointing Aaron and his sons so that they could minister to God in their priestly office. They did not have the ability and the know-how to operate as priests until they were anointed (divinely empowered).

The recipe for the holy oil as prescribed by God to Moses was established with copyright restrictions and was not to be duplicated by unauthorized persons. This holy anointing oil was made up of five ingredients blended together: pure myrrh, sweet cinnamon, sweet calamus, cassia, and olive oil. These are all natural extracts which are most useful when crushed, squeezed, or bruised. For instance, myrrh, a yellowish gummy liquid extracted from its thorny shrub, makes an excellent spice or ointment. In the same way both the cassia and cinnamon oil are gleaned from the bark of trees. Cassia may be used as medicine by a doctor and the cinnamon makes for a superb food flavoring. Calamus, on the other hand, oozes a sweet fragrance when crushed and broken. Finally, once the fruit on the olive tree is ripe, the olive is placed under extreme pressure so that the oil may be extracted.

The five products for the holy oil and the processes they undergo are symbolic of the coming forth of humanity's spiritual anointing, but the pressing of the natural olive provides the most vivid picture. The same kind of preparation needed for an olive to become oil transpires in the lives of God's chosen vessels. In fact, it is the bruising that ushers us into a higher level of anointing and enables us to be true witnesses of the true and living God who specializes in mending broken lives and restoring crushed hopes.

The holy oil that was made in the days of Moses carried with it certain restrictions; it could not be applied to a non-Israelite (i.e., the "stranger" of Exodus 30:33). Such limitations excluded many and placed a barrier on who was qualified to operate in the anointing. This is not a foreign practice; unfortunately even today in the twenty-first century, if certain persons could have the final say, many would be denied the privilege of operating in God's anointing. In some of our Christian communities there is a hidden book of reference as to who can flow and operate in the anointing. As a Christian I am often annoyed at the "Sunday movie stars," better known as Sunday anointed folks. These persons love to sit as near to the front pew as possible, are the first to testify, know when to raise their hands in praise, and can even force tears at the appropriate moment. They are the ones seen as the anointed, called out by God; but unfortunately, on Saturdays these are often the same ones that can be found in the disco or sitting at the local bar. On weekdays you might hear them arguing and fighting with their spouses or family members. As we read in the Book of Exodus, I am so glad that it was God who decided who was to be anointed; because we humans generally only see outer appearances and miss the true genuine heart requirement.

Jesus clothed Himself in human flesh, died on Calvary's cross, and rose from the dead three days later. This selfless act of His replaced the Old Testament anointing with the holy oil with being anointed by the Holy Spirit. According to Bible scholars the number five (the number of ingredients in the anointing oil) represents the grace of God, which is God's unmerited favor. By God's grace men and women alike are empowered by His Spirit (anointing) to help reconcile humanity back to Him (God).

Hence, it does not matter how people try to render you unqualified for God's anointing; they will not be able to stop the flow of anointing in your life. It is God who steps into our midst and pours the holy oil (Holy Spirit, anointing, grace) upon us so that it flows continuously with no interference from our opponents. You might be feeling discouraged because you have been overlooked for a position in your church for many years. Well, find strength in knowing that when the time is fully come, the mercy and grace of God supersedes church dogma and favoritism. You are going through that (whatever you are experiencing) so God can bring you into this (your awesome future). Remember, the spices that are blended to make up the anointing oil are both bitter and sweet, and the olive oil binds them all together.

My friend it's your bittersweet experiences that are going to take you from glory to glory. Remember, "no pain no gain." It is your pain that's going to produce unusual results.

Anointed by the Spirit of God

The anointing of the Spirit of God was made available to us through Christ's suffering, death, burial, resurrection, and ascension. Christ experienced both bitter and sweet moments in His earthly ministry. Jesus Christ's Gethsemane experience made the anointing available to His church. Gethsemane means oil press or a place of pressing. Therefore, because the anointing oil was pressed out of Christ who is the Anointed One, God's anointing for His church is now available for His chosen vessels. Those who will pay the price of suffering will be recipients of this anointing. The Old Testament holy anointing oil was representative of the Holy Spirit of God; whereas in the Old Testament they were anointed by the holy anointing oil, in the New Testament we are anointed directly by the Holy Spirit. The holy anointing oil—the archetype of the Spirit of God resting upon them in days of old—was God's approval and empowerment upon an individual for service. Notice that the anointing by the holy anointing oil would then qualify the vessel for the Spirit to not *abide in* them but *rest upon* them to carry out a specific task.

In the days of old, the Holy Spirit (anointing of God) rested upon them, giving them supernatural power to accomplish God's desire on earth. Immediately after this accomplishment, the anointing (Holy Spirit) would lift off of them. Samson is a clear example of this anointing (God's enabling power) resting on or anointing him for a particular assignment. The Israelites were in bondage to the Philistines for forty years. Therefore God raised up this great warrior, a man of valor and full of strength to deliver Israel from the oppression of the Philistines (see Judges 13).

Our communities are in serious warfare. The enemy has targeted them and the only way to save them is to flow in the anointing of God. Many people are trying to fight a spiritual battle with natural weapons. Like Samson, victory is imminent only to the extent that the Spirit of God rests upon us and gives us supernatural weaponry or strength to defeat our foes. While God is not the author of confusion nor does He promote evil, there are some battles that God will anoint us to fight. Samson warring with the Philistines, for instance, was continually anointed by God's Spirit resting upon him in time of need. The Bible declares the following:

> And Samson went down to Timnath, and saw a woman in Timnath of the daughters of the Philistines. And he came up, and told his father and his mother, and said, I have seen a woman in Timnath of the daughters of the Philistines: now therefore get her for me to wife. Then his father and his mother said unto him, Is there never a woman among the daughters of thy brethren, or among all my people, that thou goest to take a wife of the uncircumcised Philistines? And Samson said unto his father, Get her for me; for she pleaseth me well. But his father and his mother knew not that it was of the LORD, that he sought an occasion against the Philistines: for at that time the Philistines had dominion over Israel. Then went Samson down, and his father and his mother, to Timnath, and came to the vineyards of Timnath: and, behold, a young lion roared against him. And the Spirit of the LORD came mightily upon him, and he rent him as he would have rent a kid, and he had

nothing in his hand: but he told not his father or his
mother what he had done.

—JUDGES 14:1–6

Notice that the Spirit (anointing, enablement) of God
came upon him for service and accomplishment. There are
many more examples of the Spirit of God coming upon
Samson to empower him for his assignments (Judg. 14:19;
15:14). So we see that the anointing (the Holy Spirit) rested
upon God's servants of old to empower them for service.
The anointing simply empowers you with unusual abilities for your God-given assignment. In the Old Testament
we find that the anointing rested upon God's servants and
when the job was completed it lifted off of them. But in
New Testament times the anointing (Holy Spirit) of God
indwells in His people for instant and for continued service.

The great apostle John declares: "But the anointing which
ye have received of him abideth in you, and ye need not that
any man teach you: but as the same anointing teacheth you
of all things, and is truth, and is no lie, and even as it hath
taught you, ye shall abide in him" (1 John 2:27). It may
be inferred from John's writing that in the New Testament
church the anointing *abides in* them, rather than *rests upon*
them. The anointing, the supernatural divine enablement of
God, abides in His servants in this dispensation. Therefore,
no longer will it be the holy anointing oil of former times
only used for a certain few.

Although grace is the key component for the outpouring
of such anointing, the element of holiness is still a must for
any vessel to be used to house such an anointing. Many
folks would have you to believe that you can live any kind
of way and still operate in the holy anointing. As with the
holy oil in Moses' day, God is still requiring a standard of

holiness to be met. The psalmist declared in Psalm 92:10, "But my horn shalt thou exalt like the horn of a unicorn: I shall be anointed [empowered] with fresh oil." The unicorn is a symbol of power and strength. The anointing is God's power and strength working for Him through us, His set aside (sanctified, sacred, holy) vessels.

For Samson and many others like him, the anointing (the Spirit of God) rested upon them to complete a task and once the task was completed the anointing lifted. However, in this hour God's chosen vessels are carriers of the anointing.

CARRIERS OF THE ANOINTING

In days of old kings, priests and prophets alike experienced the holy anointing oil of God that equipped them for service. In the Book of Exodus, Aaron and his sons were specifically named for a special anointing. Thus, in this section it is implied that an anointing (smearing or pouring on of oil or other substance) is different from the anointed (the vessel used to carry the anointing). The actual carrier of the anointing has special powers to transform lives. The writing found in the Gospel of Luke explains this better.

> The Spirit of the LORD is upon Me, Because He has anointed Me To preach the gospel to the poor; He has sent Me to heal the brokenhearted; To proclaim liberty to the captives And recovery of sight to the blind, To set at liberty those who are oppressed; To proclaim the acceptable year of the LORD.
> —LUKE 4:18–19, NKJV

Here Jesus is saying in order for me to preach, heal, deliver, give sight to the blind and to liberate those who are captive, I must be empowered by the Holy Spirit (anointed).

The anointing is not for selfish gain or self-centered ideals or only for a special clique. Rather the anointing is a reservoir of hope and healing for the outcast and ostracized.

David was a mere shepherd boy when God anointed him with a kingly anointing. If you would recall, David was out in the fields when Samuel the prophet came on an assignment to anoint a king (see 1 Samuel 16:1–13). We can glean some important points from this anointing ceremony. Firstly, what God has ordained for us to have, we shall have as long as we stay in position. No matter who shows up or how physically fit our opponents may appear in men's eyes—David was seen as a dirty little shepherd boy—at the end of the day God is still God. Secondly, God does not make mistakes; the brothers looked more suited for kingship because of their outward appearance but God looked inwardly for a pure heart. Thirdly, a physical anointing does not mandate a speedy course to the palace or the task assigned (i.e., David was anointed but not appointed until years later). The carriers of such anointing must use it wisely, not for popularity or to gain riches or power. In many, many instances the carriers of the anointing evolve from humble beginnings and the longevity of the anointing rests upon the carrier's ability to remain humble. Pride is a weapon of mass destruction when placed alongside the anointing. God declared through His eagle-eye prophet Isaiah: "I am the Lord; that is my name: and my glory will I not give to another, neither my praise to graven images" (Isa. 42:8). Hence, the anointing of God is designed merely to equip us for service to others and to bring total glory to God.

Many persons refuse to operate in their call of God due to a lack of confidence in themselves and their abilities. Well, once God has called us we can be sure that He will equip us. The anointing will qualify the unqualified. When I was first called into ministry, I barely knew how to pray, much less preach a sermon. But the more the anointing began to flow in my life, the more skilled I became. As I look back over the years, I realize that it could only have been the grace (unmerited favor) of God that instructed, qualified, and sealed me for ministry. Remember, what God calls for, He will provide for. We must trust God to do the work in and through us. When we look only at our gifting, then sure we are bound to fail. But when we look to the all-knowing, all-sufficient God, then victory will be the final deal. God has a supernatural anointing with your name on it. This anointing will equip you to help usher in the end-time harvest. Are you willing to pay the price for it?

The anointing oil described to Moses was not to be poured upon strangers (those who were not ordained for it) nor was it to be imitated or substituted. Thank God there is no substitute because the church is becoming more and more filled with people who are copycats. For example, if Mary sang under a powerful anointing last Sunday, three or four other sisters who do not have the gift of singing will fight to get the microphone the next Sunday for the opportunity to do it the way it was done by Mary. Why are we limiting God to a particular movement? God will show up in many forms and still provide an anointing that will bless our socks off each time. We have to stay in our calling and let God use us for His glory. The anointing is not manufactured or duplicated; any efforts to fabricate the anointing could result in annihilation of your present gifting. Either you have it or you don't.

I was once told by a good friend that you don't know what you have until you need what you had. The anointing is costly, valuable, expensive, and rare; and once you have been endowed by this power, guard it and don't lose it because you will need it. Dr. Mike Murdock once said that a fish in its environment (the water) is a genius (mastermind). I will say that a man or woman operating in their God-ordained calling and anointing is capable of doing anything that their God desires of them. These carriers of the anointing are what I call spiritual masterminds. The anointing sanctifies all, setting all apart for God's purpose.

People will often try to get you to move out of position, but you have to maintain your ground; do not move; you've been set apart. Stay in the environment of glory, the presence of God, and see what God will do through you. In these times we are living in, whether we are nobles or peasants, we need the supernatural anointing of God (God's enabling power). Any task we must undertake (physical, mental, or spiritual) will require us to function at a higher level to achieve success. Moreover, God deems us to be a royal people (kingly); hence, He requires us to operate with a certain stamina and excellence. We are at our best and able to "rub shoulders" with men of high esteem when the anointing is flowing in and through us. The apostle Paul declared in Philippians 4:13, "I can do all things through Christ which strengtheneth me." You are a carrier of God's anointing.

In biblical times anyone who was anointed with the holy anointing oil was known as God's anointed. The holy anointing oil is symbolic of the ministry of the Holy Spirit. That is, it has a similar ability to quicken and illuminate with power upon the one who is anointed. Like I stated earlier, the anointing cannot be imitated. The Bible declares in Romans 11:29: "For the gifts and calling of God are without repentance." There are many persons that are in the body of Christ operating in gifts that are not empowered by the anointing; therefore, there are no lasting results. You cannot fake the anointing; either you have it or you don't.

It doesn't make sense to covet someone else's anointing; if you were not pressed (suffered) to the measure that they were pressed, the anointing tailor-made for them will only destroy you. The vessels of God's anointing must be built to house the power. In other words, you must be properly wired to sustain the level of power (anointing) that God allows to flow through your life. Remember, the anointing is the supernatural, divine enablement of God for His chosen vessels. God on flesh and working through and in flesh doing only what God can do is the anointing.

> The anointing is the supernatural, divine enablement of God for His chosen vessels.

Chapter Two

THE VESSEL

THE VESSEL DEFINED

GOD USES ORDINARY people to do extraordinary things for His glory by filling them (the vessel) with His Holy Spirit. Thus, humanity becomes the agent of God's grace and the vehicle of His power, love, healing, and mercy to flow through to a hurting and dying world. The word *vessel* is a container used for holding something. This container may take the form of a barrel, bottle, bowl, or cup; or it can be a person who is viewed as the holder or recipient of a tangible or intangible quality (for example, grace, love, wealth, material goods, or some special skill). In some Christian forums the word *vessel* is used to refer to a person who is anointed by God (called a carrier of the anointing). Whether we know it or not, we are all vessels; for hidden deep within us is a container ready to be filled to overflowing with the mandate or Spirit of God.

God uses ordinary people to do extraordinary things for His glory...

There is an unusual anointing God wants to pour out in these last days, but He needs some prepared and available vessels to carry it: Those who will take up their cross and follow Him (Matt. 16:24). The Bible declares: "But there is a spirit in man; and the inspiration of the Almighty giveth them understanding" (Job 32:8). First of all, the Bible is saying here that even though there is a spirit in every man (the vessel), it is the inspiration of the Almighty (i.e., the Spirit of the Almighty) that gives them (the vessel) the understanding, knowledge, anointing, and direction. The word *inspiration* here comes from the Hebrew word *neshamah*, which means breathe, divine intellect (divine in telling), spirit, or enlightenment (Strong's #5397). So we see here that God's Spirit breathes into man (the vessel), giving him supernatural ability and power to do supernatural things here on earth for the kingdom. Therefore, God needs men and women who have made themselves available to be used by Him. Are you willing to pay the price?

I recall during my childhood when confronted by bullies and/or arrogant, boastful students, we would often chant: "Empty vessels make the most noise." In essence we were predicting that these persons had nothing but hot air in them and their fruitless claims/threats were derived from the emptiness that filled them up on the inside. So it is the same without the Holy Spirit; we are nothing but empty vessels making the most noise, lacking true power and love. Once we make ourselves available to God to be used as a vessel, He then fashions us and breathes His Spirit into us, which empowers us for service. The Bible declares, "God is a Spirit" (John 4:24). And the apostle Paul also declares, "Now the Lord is that Spirit" (2 Cor. 3:17). We can clearly see from these two passages of scripture that God is indeed a Spirit. In order for a spirit to operate to accomplish God's divine plans here on earth, it must have a body. The Holy Spirit needs a vessel (body); and not just any vessel but a prepared vessel. As the apostle Paul notes, He needs "a vessel unto honour, sanctified, and meet for the master's use, and prepared unto every good work" (2 Tim. 2:21). God is in search of vessels, men and women whom He can pour His Spirit (anointing) upon.

CALLED TO BE A VESSEL

God chooses those who have been processed through His orchestrated mentoring fire and have come out as pure gold. These will be the vessels chosen to harness this unusual hundredfold anointing in these last days. In the past, many persons have offered themselves to faithfully serve in the church; but after a while they have given up because of opposition, pain, and, of course, pressure. It appears that these vessels that fell by the way did not go through the refining process. Perhaps they came out of the mentoring fire prematurely.

In this day God is calling persons who are willing to endure to the end. Yes, God realizes that in our own strength and power we cannot survive; hence, He has sent the Comforter, the Holy Spirit, to dwell within us (John 14:16). Maybe for a long time you have felt that God is calling you but through your own insecurities you have brushed those feelings aside. Or perhaps you are not sure of God's call upon your life. I believe that as God called from the portals of heaven to earth to the Christian leaders of old times, He is calling for you and I to be vessels used for His glory.

A person carries the anointing not for personal glory but that Jesus Christ might be glorified. In God's kingdom the humble are exalted while the proud are abased. Jesus told His disciples that in order to be exalted and become great they must become "faceless" (not wanting to be seen). We need to just stay humble and serve God and others and God will do the impossible. God will only use humble vessels in this season, those who will not take advantage of His precious people. Remember, power in the hands of the wrong person (vessel) can birth catastrophic results. Atomic power can generate light and heat for a whole city or it can be dropped as a bomb on that same city to its destruction. Likewise, laser power directed in proper timing and proportion can perform surgery to bring healing or it can be used as a weapon to destroy. The power carriers (the vessels) in this final outpouring will be those who are willing and obedient (humble) to every command from the Commander and Chief.

God will only use a vessel that has been on His potter's wheel. In the Book of Jeremiah, chapter 18, we find the story of the potter and the clay. Jeremiah was told by the Lord to rise up and go down to the potter's house. Upon his arrival at the potter's house, Jeremiah met the potter making a vessel; but the vessel was marred (damaged, disfigured) that he had made. Jeremiah says in verse 4 that he made another vessel. There is much to be learned from this production. First, the potter does not hesitate to rework the pottery. Also, while he rejects what was made, he does not discard the materials used to make it. There are times in our Christian walk where we feel that we have made such huge mistakes that God could never use us. While God is not pleased with sin, He removes them from us (Ps. 103:12), and He still longs to restore us and use us for His glory.

God will only use a vessel that has been on His potter's wheel.

The potter takes the same clay and makes a different vessel. Like the potter, God takes the rejects, murderers, robbers, drug pushers, drug addicts, whoremongers, high school dropouts, and the unqualified and remakes them on His potter's wheel into vessels of honor, fit for the Master's use.

The apostle Paul, for example, was a special vessel that God had to reform on His potter's wheel. Saul, whose name was changed to Paul, persecuted the believers; yet he was predestined by God to be an apostle (vessel) to the Gentiles. It's important to note that a man's broken past has very little to do with God's ability to transform him into a dazzling vessel. As mentioned in Acts 8:3, Saul made havoc in the church by imprisoning those who professed faith in Jesus as Christ. He even threatened and actually slaughtered many of Jesus' followers. However, he was eventually converted on the way to Damascus, and God placed him on the potter's wheel.

This same persecutor and murderer who consented to Stephen's death was transformed into a vessel of light which shined brightly for Jesus Christ. The disciples did not accept him at first because of his past. But it did not matter what they thought because God had big plans for Paul's (the former Saul) future. Earlier the disciples were trying to find a substitute apostle for Judas among the brethren, but God had placed this position upon Paul. He was the chosen vessel, not by men but by God. You see humanity does not have the authority to transfer the anointing. It is God who selects who He wants to carry out a particular task.

Over the years, the church has suffered greatly because

leaders have been handpicking persons and "assigning" an anointing on them for particular positions in the church; this anointing never arrived upon these man-picked vessels. We have persons in the church who should be singing so softly that no one hears them, yet in special services they are handed the microphone to sing the lead part in the choir. Of course there is the oh so popular generational preachers' marathon where the father hands the church to his son who is not saved and has no intention of getting saved. The house of God is in disarray because people are not asking God for proven vessels; they are picking up the clay that is still on the potter's wheel, that hasn't been in the fire, and making bishops. There is more to the anointing than the smearing on of olive oil, having elaborate ordination services, and the laying on of hands. God Himself must breathe into our spirit.

In Acts 1:15–26 we are told how the eleven apostles cast lots to replace Judas Iscariot, who betrayed Jesus and then hung himself. The lot fell on Matthias and he was officially a disciple. This did not hinder the work that God had called Paul to do. In fact, the results of Paul's labor among the Greek proved that he was a super apostle like the others. It is so ironic that Paul, God's chosen vessel, is widely spoken of in the Scriptures while Matthias is only spoken of in Acts 1:23 and 26, where he is chosen by casting lots. Man's choice is almost always not God's choice. When God selects you to be His vessel, you can be sure that those around you will know that His hands are upon you. When God takes you off the potter's wheel and sets you on display, you can be sure that your contribution to those around you will be great. There is a difference between God's choice and man's choice. God's choice brings a hundredfold anointing while man's choice brings empty praises and vainglory. You can be chosen by man but not anointed by God.

Man's choice is almost always not God's choice.

A Vessel in the Making

Despite popular belief, there is a process that we must undergo in order to become a vessel of God. For example, when we offer ourselves to God for service, we come broken, scared, and stained. Hence, God purifies; chisels, and reshapes us into a vessel fit for His use. The psalmist David alludes to this as he cries:

> Behold I was shapen in iniquity; and in sin did my mother conceived me. Behold, thou desirest truth in the inward parts: and in the hidden part thou shalt make me know wisdom. Purge me with hyssop, and I shall be clean: wash me, and I shall be whiter than snow.
>
> —Psalm 51:5–7

I infer that David was saying to God, "I need to be prepared for kingship because I was formed in iniquity and conceived in sin." David's encounter with Uriah's wife made him acutely aware of his inadequacies and inability to be a true vessel of God. However, once God purged, cleansed, and washed David (took him through His mentoring fire), he was whiter than snow. Like David, God wants to polish our vessels so it can be fit for the Master's service.

Too many people rush into ministry but have not gone through the fire (testing) nor have they been tried. Hence, many find themselves unable to stand when the trials of life come their way. My friend, preparation must take place before we can carry the anointing. David didn't just wake up one day and walk into the palace to be crowned king. No, he went through the hard knocks of life by combating with wild animals while shepherding and experiencing rejection and abandonment by his brothers. David paid a heavy price for the anointing. Yes, there is a price to be paid in order to carry this powerful hundredfold anointing. Are you willing to pay the price? We will explore the revelation of the thirtyfold, sixtyfold, and hundredfold anointing in chapter 4.

The apostle Paul declared:

> What! know ye not that your body is the temple of the Holy Ghost which is in you, which ye have of God, and ye are not your own? For ye are bought with a price: therefore glorify God in your body, and in your spirit, which are God's.
>
> —1 CORINTHIANS 6:19–20

Here, we see the apostle Paul telling the saints in Corinth that their body is the temple (house, vessel) of the Holy Ghost (the anointing, Spirit of God). Are you truly willing to be a carrier of God's anointing? There is a price!

The vessels that God is seeking in this hour are not only available vessels but also humble vessels with an attitude of servanthood; ready to serve God and His people. In the Book of Matthew, chapter 23, Jesus was speaking to a multitude along with His disciples concerning the scribes and Pharisees (religious leaders) of that day. Jesus strongly rebuked them for their hypocrisy, for they were experts at putting on an outward show to be seen of men while the inside of their hearts were infected with evil.

Religious leaders today are not that much different from those mentioned here. The ongoing battle for title and power in our churches has taken the focus off of God and placed it on man. Many leaders have been deceived by the devil into thinking that the title of reverend, bishop, apostle, prophet, or pastor automatically transfers the anointing. And so they strive for these man-made accolades and neglect getting into the presence of God. Society dictates to Christian leaders that the anointing can only flow from a certain set of people, those whose outward appearances (carefully woven robes, other priestly attire, and sanctimonious demeanor) suggest that they are carriers of the anointing. Unfortunately, the Scriptures seem to imply something quite opposite to this. Like Jesus alluded to in Matthew 23, those persons desirous of honorary status and recognition in public spectrums do not qualify to carry this end-time anointing. The vessels that God will empower are clean on the outside as well as on the inside.

Types of vessels

Whenever God has a specific assignment to be carried out, He will prepare a unique vessel to house the anointing that will be needed for that special assignment. There are several types of vessels that will be needed for that special assignment, including the following:

- **Chosen Vessel:** The Greek word for "chosen" is *eklego*, and it means to chose for oneself; one who has been foreordained, predetermined, predestined, and sanctified (set aside) by God for a specific task (purpose).

- **Yielded Vessel:** The Hebrew word for "yield" is *gevurah*, and it means to give up, as to superior power or authority; one who has surrendered all to God—spirit, soul, mind, and body—with the cry, "Father, not my will but thine be done."

- **Tested Vessel:** The Greek word for "tested" is *peirazo*, and it means to prove, to test, or to try; one who has been tried by the fire (various trials and tribulations) and came forth as pure gold.

- **Vessel of Honor:** The Hebrew word for "honor" is *kabad*, and it means to be heavy, weighty, rich, honorable, and glorious; one who has been chosen, yielded, tested, and is now fit and meet for the master's use. God's honored vessel now brings true glory to their God.

A Vessel Hidden in God

In the natural, some vessels (inanimate objects) are costly and thus precious and must be protected from damage. The fragility of certain vessels may force the owner to place them on display in a secure area for fear that to use them would damage the vessel. God has not chosen us to be display pieces that are only dust collectors at the end of the day. God has set us aside to be employed by Him to be fully functional and used. You don't have to be confused by the arrows of the enemy; you are a chosen vessel, and God has you shielded from the destroyer. In the Book of Jeremiah God assures the prophet Jeremiah that He will be with him throughout his assignments. In fact, God reminds Jeremiah that before he was in the womb He had chosen him (see Jeremiah 1:5). This same seal that God placed upon Jeremiah from the onset is upon your life. My friend, God placed you in your mother's womb because He needed a vessel for a specific task here on earth. And guess what? None of your jealous opponents can house the anointing that was prepared specifically for you to carry out your special assignment. I must remind you, though, that after physical birth each vessel must be prepared, and for the most part it is by God's orchestrated mentoring fire (trials).

In the case of Jeremiah, for example, God needed a vessel to tell the people of Judah and Jerusalem that He was sending the families of the kingdom of the North to punish them because they had become wicked. They had turned from Him and were burning incense unto other gods and worshipping the works of their own hands (Jer. 1:15–16). God needed someone to be His mouthpiece to herald His warnings to the Israelites. For this reason, God selected Jeremiah (a vessel) to carry His prophetic anointing.

I would like to point out this truth to you: God lives in eternity and we, His people, live in time. God looked from eternity into time and saw the evil that His people in Judah and Jerusalem were doing and He decided to warn them but knew He would need a vessel (prophet) to speak through. Reflect on the increasing moral decay in the world, the loss of love and care for others, the fighting within and without, suffering of all sorts, natural disasters, etc. Surely, even now in the days in which we are living, God still needs a mouthpiece, hands, feet, and eyes to bring peace, love, and care back to humanity. God needs a vessel like you.

Maybe, like Jeremiah, you are saying, "But I am too young" or "I can't speak" or "I lack the skills needed to serve." God knows your abilities or lack thereof, and He knows that after preparation you will be a force to be reckoned with. In fact, as the Bible declares in reference to Jeremiah, God continues to say to us, "Before I formed thee in the belly [a physical body, the vessel] I knew thee; and before thou camest forth out of the womb [physical birth] I sanctified [set you apart] thee, and I ordained thee a prophet [special vessel] unto the nations" (Jer. 1:5). Before mother and father came together, God knew that there would be a Jeremiah. And likewise He also knew that there would be a you. It was God who placed Jeremiah, His chosen vessel, in his mother's womb so he could carry out His predetermined plans here on earth. God was at work long before Jeremiah was conceived, shaping the very thought of his conception to fall in line with his actual life span. God knows you, so refrain from complaining and making excuses but rather commit to becoming a vessel that is fit and ready for the Master's use. God will take your insecurities and your shortcomings and He will furnish you with the skills needed for the task. As the writer alludes to in the Book of Jeremiah 18, God is like a potter and we are like the clay. He molds and remolds us until we are fit for His purpose.

We spend too much time competing with each other or fighting to fit in with the crowd or lobbying for positions in church. We lose sight of what God really has designed us for. Once God has a call on your life, there is absolutely nothing that anyone in heaven or earth can do to stop God from fulfilling His will. You are the only one who can delay or frustrate the plans of God for your life. Stop worrying about those ferocious and atrocious enemies; they will try but they can't stop the flow of God in your life. God has placed His seal upon you, so hold your head high and carry on the work that God has set for you to do. Many will come with man's approval and recommendation trying to replace you in the kingdom, but don't stress; they are just wasting their time. No one can walk in your shoes; they will either be too big or too small, too wide or too narrow for them. Remember, what God has for you, it is for you.

I know you sometimes feel like nothing is working in your favor and as if the enemy is having his way. My friend, it is not so; God is in control. And whether you believe it or not, you are right on schedule, you have been hidden to be revealed. God knows, not man, what shoes He wants for your feet; and in due season, like the story of Cinderella, you will step out to the ball and steal the heart of the Prince. For what God has for you, it is for you.

Just as the potter in the Book of Jeremiah took the marred (blemished, flawed, stained, disfigured) vessel and made it into another vessel, likewise God will do with each of us. Like the potter, God will make us over as many times as is deemed necessary; the end result will be maximum success. We tend to get very anxious when God puts us back on the wheel, but there is no need to fear; God, the Master Potter, knows our frame and He is quite aware of our durability. The crushing of the clay (trials and testing) may appear destructive, and sometimes we might wonder if we will ever come out as a vessel of honor. Just endure the remolding for the latter is going to be greater than the former. If God gave us a peek at the end results, we would easily be able to rejoice during the crushing blows of life. Nevertheless, God assures us in His Word that we are destined for greatness; we just have to trust Him to shape us for our destiny. Just remember, you have been hidden, waiting to be revealed.

Unlike today where we are prone to select those we feel are the most favored, talented, educated, and sophisticated as the mighty ones of God, God chooses people who are unqualified in age, gender, academics, speech, and so forth to carry the anointing and to be vessels of honor. God hides His special vessels right in the midst of the sophisticated and the educated even while preparation is taking place. What an awesome God! Even while they are not aware of it, God's powerful transformations and metamorphoses are taking place, catapulting those who are last (vessels of honor) to the place of that of the seemingly first (society-chosen vessel). Each vessel that God chooses carries a specific anointing for a specific task that only it can fulfill. For example, when God needed a man to begin the human race, He chose Adam. When He needed an ark, He chose Noah to construct it. When He wanted a special lineage of people, He chose Abraham. When He needed to feed His people during a famine, He chose Joseph. When He needed to deliver His people out of Egypt, He chose Moses. When He wanted to take them over into Canaan, He chose Joshua. When He wanted to do a "new thing" in Israel, He chose Samuel. When He wanted prophetic voices in Israel, He chose Isaiah, Jeremiah, Ezekiel, Daniel, etc. When He needed a forerunner for Christ, He chose John the Baptist. And when He needed a Savior for the world, He chose His only begotten Son, Jesus. Those who will carry this power-packed hundredfold anointing will pass through God's assembly line (His orchestrated mentoring process) coming out on the other side as vessels of honor, equipped, fit, steady, and ready for the Master's use. Again I ask, are you willing to pay the price?

Chapter Three

PAYING THE PRICE

THE PRICE OF THE ANOINTING IS GREAT!

WHILE SOME MAY view the anointing on your life as common, I imagine you paid a significant price to get to the place where you are spiritually. The anointing upon an individual varies according to the things he or she has suffered and the price they have paid. It is natural to desire the gifting of great persons; and in some aspects, these gifts are obtainable, but are you willing to pay the price? In Matthew 20:20, the story is told of the mother of Jesus' disciples James and John. This woman was convinced that her sons were qualified to reign with Jesus. In fact, the sons felt they deserved it because they had left everything and followed him (Luke 5:11).

The anointing upon an individual varies according to the things he or she has suffered and the price they have paid.

Mark reports it this way: "Grant us that we may sit," said the sons of Zebedee, "one on Your right hand and the other on Your left, in Your glory" (Mark 10:37, NKJV). Isn't that just like us today? Looking to occupy the chief seat and to be recognized by flamboyant titles? Jesus asked those hungry for power and prestige: "Are you able to drink from the cup that I drink?" (v. 38, NKJV). One would think the response would have been in the form of the question: "Well, what all is in that cup Jesus?" Rather, the sons said, "We can" (v. 39). They had signed up for the glory of it all, not the humiliation (the cost). Like many of us, Zebedee's sons wanted the spiritual gifts, the reward, and the glory. They expected to eat the heavenly food and live forever. While these made up a small portion of the ingredients in Jesus' cup, there was much more.

The cup that Jesus drank held betrayal by a trusted companion (Matt. 26:48). Jesus was abandoned by God (Matt. 27:46), brutalized by the government of that day (Matt. 27:28–31), and forsaken by His friends (Matt. 26:56); yet, He took His cup (the price of atonement for us all) in hand and drank it. Earlier we find Jesus in Gethsemane, with sweats of blood crying, "O my Father, if it be possible, let this cup pass from me: nevertheless not as I will, but as thou wilt" (Matt. 26:39). Will you really be able to drink from that cup?

James and John had a caring mother who wanted the best for them, including having them to sit in high places. She asked Jesus to grant her request, and He asked whether they would able to drink of the cup of suffering, the precursor to the greater anointing. Everybody wants to be used by God in a mighty way but few want to pay the price of the pain, suffering, rejection, persecution, isolation, criticism, lack, etc., that comes with it. The hundredfold anointing may even cost you your life. Are you willing to pay the price?

There is a fairly common saying: Everybody wants to go to heaven but nobody wants to die. How very true this statement is, even in the life of the most committed Christians. Yes, everyone wants to experience God's heavenly glory and power but no one wants to die to the flesh to receive it. The Bible declares in John 12:24: "Verily, verily, I say unto you, Except a corn of wheat fall into the ground and die, it abideth alone: but if it die, it bringeth forth much fruit."

A RARE COMMODITY

In April 2008 I had the awesome privilege to tour the Holy Land with Dr. Myles Munroe, President of Bahamas Faith Ministries. At the end of one of our tour days, we were given the option to visit a diamond factory or return to the hotel. I, along with several others, opted to explore the diamond factory. As we exited the bus, Dr. Munroe stuck his head out of the window of the bus, which was now heading to the hotel, and said, "Are you sure you want to go in there?" Preoccupied by the thought of exploring the factory, I brushed off his comments and headed for the entrance to the factory.

Wow, that was surely the most beautiful site in the jewelry world! To take one or two pieces from there, my friend, would seal the deal to your wife's heart. (Aren't diamonds a girl's best friend?) However, Dr. Munroe's words soon returned to haunt me as I observed the price labels on the diamonds. Diamond rings, bracelets, and chains were priced from thirty to forty thousand dollars. The number of persons in our group soon dwindled. Some folks went outside (possibly to catch their breath from the shocking prices) while others returned to the hotel. Are you willing to pay the price?

Many persons come into ministry with good intentions

of sticking it out to the end. The power to endure is found only when we are willing to go behind the veil into the presence of God and remain there. It is there that the greater gain of oil is found. It seems, however, that once people become knowledgeable of the price to be paid for the greater gain, they decided to give up, calling the journey too difficult. Like some of the persons on our tour, many decide to go outside and wait for the bus, to go back to mediocrity. Ironically, some of the folks that retreat are the very ones that will become jealous of those who stayed and paid the price. Just like the diamonds, the hundredfold anointing is brilliant, beautiful, costly, and powerful. To possess it you must be willing to pay the price. You can be sure that the one receiving it (the diamond or anointing) will wear it with pride and honor. It was hard to appreciate the price but there is authenticity in the pricing.

What is a diamond? According to Webster New World Dictionary, "A diamond is a nearly pure, colorless, crystalline carbon, the hardest mineral, used as gems or cutting tools." In other words, diamonds are the crystallized form of carbon created under extreme heat and pressure. This same process makes diamonds the hardest mineral known. Just like diamonds, the hundredfold anointing is only released upon a chosen vessel that has also been through extreme heat and pressure. Are you willing to pay the price? Diamonds require specific geological conditions to form and are only found in certain locations. Likewise, the supernatural power (hundredfold anointing) that will come upon a God-selected people (the remnant) will require a "stay over" in God's prescribed environment overflowing with His orchestrated mentoring trials. Like the natural diamonds, this hundredfold anointing requires specific geological conditions to come forth. Be prepared to go through some rough times and to make some unpopular decisions and to walk some lonely roads; it's all in the geological climate.

REAL VERSUS COUNTERFEIT

There is a remnant that God has preserved for such a time as this. As I was meditating on what and who this could be, I began to reflect on the similarities to the diamonds. As diamonds are found only in certain locations, even so those who will house this power-packed anointing will be found only in strategic places. They will be God's CIA (Central Intelligence Agency) and FBI (Federal Bureau of Investigation) agents: God's specialists. Carriers of the anointing are specially designed and equipped for the Master's service. The uniqueness of these gems will allow them to be distinguished from copies or prototypes. The ability to duplicate such rare commodities will be extinguished because every vessel will have unique qualities that cannot be dressed on another.

Of course, just as there are different sizes, shapes, colors, and looks of diamonds, so there are different kinds of anointing. There are both natural and man-made diamonds. Which will you prefer? The natural that comes from God or the superficial that comes from man?

So it leads me to ask another question: Are you operating in God's anointing or man's anointing? If you are working hard to preach, prophesy, sing, or to accomplish that which you claim to be anointed for, then chances are you may be operating in man's anointing. So many are operating in man's anointing and have settled for man's power rather than God's power. All it took was for someone to pour oil on their head in the midst of a great multitude and declare for them a position in God's kingdom that God didn't know anything about; therefore, there is no unction (anointing) to function.

If you have answered the call because someone "felt" that you would make a good apostle, prophet, bishop, pastor, etc.—as opposed to you feeling and God revealing His call on your life—then chances are it's man-made. If your desire is to gain man's approval as opposed to God's, then you are missing the mark. God's anointing *makes it happen* for the kingdom. The ones anointed by God desire the things of God; and, in fact, the zeal for God's house will consume them. Remember, the real deal is birthed out of the fire. Are you willing to pay the price?

Natural diamonds are produced from microorganisms (organisms too small to be viewed) that lived and died in the ocean and then eventually fell to the ocean floor. What is left of the decomposed state of these bodies is pure carbon. The carbon eventually becomes buried under tons of rocks, causing it to be subject to extreme pressure by the rock pressing down upon it and extreme heat, which is usually between 1,100 and 1,400 degrees Celsius. This will then cause a metamorphosis (a complete change of form) to take place, changing the carbon to a crystallized stone called a diamond. These natural diamonds will surface to the top every once and a while when a volcano erupts.

Natural diamonds are much more costly than man-made diamonds. Why? It is because of the process which it takes to come forth. As the apostle Peter said:

> Beloved, think it not strange concerning the fiery trail which is to try you, as though some strange thing happened unto you: But rejoice, inasmuch as ye are partakers of Christ's sufferings; that, when

His glory shall be revealed, ye may be glad also with exceeding joy.

—1 Peter 4:12–13

Peter is saying that although the trials that will come your way bring great suffering, they will eventually qualify you for the anointing (hundredfold anointing) and thus should not to be considered strange. Why? It is the price that has to be paid to partake in God's glory.

There are also man-made diamonds that may look like the real thing but are not. These diamonds are developed using a similar process as the natural diamonds. Pure carbon is placed under enough heat and pressure to crystallize into a hard gem. Then much-needed chemicals are added which eventually produce man-made diamonds. Most of the time these man-made diamonds are yellow and not clear like the natural diamonds. But at times man-made diamonds look so much like the natural diamonds that only trained jewelers can tell the difference.

The authenticity of the diamonds can be detected by the growth pattern of the diamonds or the lack of inclusions (tiny bits of material that are usually imbedded in the natural diamonds). So many persons in the body of Christ have settled for the look-alike; they have settled for a man-made anointing. The high cost, demands, discipline, and challenges involved with achieving God's supernatural anointing have caused many to turn from pursuing God's power. They instead have opted for an easier way and are now pursuing man's power. Man's power can come from various places: degrees/certificates from theological seminaries favor with spiritual leaders, public anointing services, clerical attire, etc. These are no match for Satan and his kingdom. We must be mindful that the power of God comes through suffering, pressure, and much pain, which in the end brings forth an undeniable and unstoppable anointing. Are you willing to pay the price?

The Bible declares in Isaiah 40:5: "And the glory of the LORD shall be revealed, and all flesh shall see it together: For the mouth of the LORD hath spoken it." The prophet Isaiah said that the mouth of the Lord hath spoken it! We can be assured that once God speaks, it shall surely come to pass. My fellow brethren in this Christian race, we must broaden our shoulders and take the blows and like the apostle Paul declares: "Endure hardness, as a good soldier of Jesus Christ" (2 Tim. 2:3). The true soldiers of Jesus Christ are the ones that will carry the weapons of war (the anointing).

Among the many requirements for a diamond to be formed naturally, something must die. The microorganisms that one time lived in the ocean had to die. In a similar vein, the price of this costly anointing is death, death to the old nature in order to embrace the new nature. Hence, those attacks from your haters, family, friends, coworkers, and sometimes even your spouse; struggles with finances, colleagues, church folks, neighbors, etc.; and being lied to and about, cheated, mistreated, forsaken, rejected, and denied will all work together for our betterment by killing our fleshly desires (old nature) while simultaneously resurrecting our (spiritual nature) to God's mandate.

GOD'S PRECIOUS GEMS

God will allow trials and tribulations to arise in our lives to put the old nature to death so that the new man will live. The apostle Paul said it so clearly, "For which cause we faint not; but though our outward man perish, yet the inward man is renewed day by day" (2 Cor. 4:16). The price to be paid for this awesome power will put our fleshy outer man under subjection while awakening an anointed power-packed inner man for kingdom exploits. Just as those dead microorganisms fell to the bottom of the ocean, even so it is required by God that our old nature do likewise in order for the new nature to reign supreme. My friends, humility is a prerequisite for this glory. James said, "Humble yourselves in the sight of the Lord, and he shall lift you up" (James 4:10). Jesus said, "He that shall humble himself shall be exalted" (Matt. 23:12). God's weight of glory, power, favor, and anointing will only rest upon those who paid the price of humility. We must put away arrogance, pride, boastfulness, haughtiness, vainglory, and even self (old nature) in order to be an effective servant in the body of Christ. This effectiveness will birth the power and anointing needed for the humble servant to fulfill God's will. You are God's precious gem!

A complete metamorphosis (change) must take place before we become who He has purposed for us to be. Contrasting the process of the microorganisms dying and falling to the bottom of the ocean to the state of remolding and reshaping to our own processes, we go through similar things before we become that beautiful diamond. The responsibility that goes with carrying the anointing will at times cost you your personal desires, plans, and will.

Jesus declared to His disciples:

> If any man will come after me, let him deny himself, and take up his cross, and follow me. For whosoever will save his life shall lose it: and whosoever will lose his life for my sake shall find it.
>
> —MATTHEW 16:24–25

Those who would be a carrier of this anointing must be willing to deny themselves, putting the kingdom of God first. This costly anointing will change your agenda; it will change your marital, friendship, financial, business, working, recreation, eating, and even your sleeping plans. It will cost you everything. But at the end of the day you will possess wonderful things. As the apostle Paul says, "Eye hath not seen, nor ear heard, neither have entered into the heart of man, the things which God hath prepared for them that love him" (1 Cor. 2:9)—anointing and favor. The level of anointing that has been prepared for those who love God enough to pay the ultimate price; but it will confound many. Trust me, there will always be a story behind the glory.

Maybe you are wondering: Why it is that you have to go through so much hardship, disappointment, and pain? Well as Theodore Rubin once said, "The problem is not that there are problems. The problem is expecting otherwise and thinking that having problems is a problem."[1] At some point in this life we will all go through some form of adversity, but our focus must not be on the fact that there are problems; rather we must concentrate on how to rise above them. Too often Christians live defeated lives because they are problem conscious. At the slightest indication of struggles we are prone to run and hide. God wants us to exercise faith in His ability to deliver us from every snare of the enemy. We already have the victory through our Lord Jesus the Christ, so there is no need to live a life of defeat. This hundred-fold anointing will bring about significant changes in your life while simultaneously causing great disturbance. Are you willing to pay the price?

Johann Paul Friedrich Richter is credited with saying, "Sleep, riches, and health, to be truly enjoyed, must be interrupted."[2] This costly anointing that brings with it great power, favor, and wealth will cause your desires, plans, and will to be interrupted for the purpose of God's kingdom. I can attest to this. When I answered God's call to ministry, I was a successful entrepreneur whose sole intention was to become wealthy. My business was booming and I was raking in thousands of dollars. This was the life for me, or so I thought. Yet God had another plan for my life; and as I embraced His plan (to harvest souls for the kingdom of heaven), I had to walk away from my plan (wealth). I concur with Dr. Mike Murdock, a mighty man of God, full of wisdom, who frequently makes this statement: "What you are willing to walk away from, will determine what God will bring you into."[3]

> This costly anointing that brings with it great power, favor, and wealth will cause your desires, plans, and will to be interrupted for the purpose of God's kingdom.

The process that the carbon goes through buried under tons of rocks subjected to the extreme pressure and heat that changes it to a diamond is also seen spiritually in the trials and testing that comes our way. Experiencing extreme pressure and heated trials is yet another pricey cost of this dynamite hundredfold anointing. Those who will harness this power-packed anointing in these last days will experience extreme pressure. It may manifest as pressure in the church because of jealous opponents, pressure of financial obligations, or pressure of family strife. It may be pressure that makes you feel like the very breath is leaving your body or pressure that at times might cause you to desire death over life. These pressures and heated situations might cause you to consider, like the great prophet Elijah, to flee and hide not even desiring food (see 1 Kings 19). But know that when it is all over, my friend, extreme pressure presses out the oil that's on the inside.

Like the olive, if it is not pressured there is no manifestation of the oil that it contains. Dr. Myles Munroe wrote a powerful book that I encourage every believer to read entitled *The Glory of Living*. In chapter 7, "Squeezing the Glory Out," Dr. Munroe says, "The full glory of a thing is not readily apparent at first glance. It is hidden beneath the surface. Glory comes out through a process that inevitably and permanently alters its container."[4]

The remnant that has been chosen by God to carry this greater anointing will be squeezed by God's pressure and filtered until they are inevitably (certainly unavoidably) and permanently changed. Isaiah 48:10 tells us: "Behold, I have refined thee, but not with silver; I have chosen thee in the furnace of affliction." The price to be paid for this anointing that will be released upon a remnant is the process of going through the furnace of affliction. The cost is also heated trials, which are unavoidable and uncontrollable. It may be a trial like flaming fire that cannot be extinguished no matter how hard you try. Are you willing to pay the price?

The price to be paid for this anointing that will be released upon a remnant is the process of going through the furnace of affliction.

There is an old African proverb that says, "Smooth seas do not make skillful sailors."[5] Likewise, smooth times do not make skillful warriors; rather it is the rough times of life that do the molding and shaping. After the carbon becomes subjected to extreme pressure and heat, it crystallizes and becomes a hard gem known as a diamond. After being fully developed, these precious gems are bound by the weight of the rocks that sit upon them until there is a volcano eruption. When the volcano erupts under the earth, the weighty rocks that held the diamonds captive are destroyed into fragments by the explosion, heat, and pressure from the eruption. As a result, the diamonds are released and surface.

Those who would endure God's orchestrated mentoring fire for the sake of preparation for the greater anointing will miraculously be released by a spiritual volcanic eruption. What is a spiritual volcanic eruption? That is when suddenly everything just goes wrong, with trouble on every side, attacks, betrayal, rejection, and so forth. As rough as these experiences may be, this is just a volcano that has erupted to bring you (God's diamond) to the top. You are about to emerge with brilliance, beauty, great value, and power to work the works of Him who called you from darkness into His marvelous light. The apostle Peter said, "Ye are a chosen generation, a royal priesthood, an holy nation, a peculiar people; that ye should show forth the praises of him who hath called you out of darkness into his marvelous light" (1 Pet. 2:9). There is a chosen generation, a special people that will dwell in His marvelous light. These are the ones who are willing to pay the price.

Chapter Four

THIRTYFOLD, SIXTYFOLD, AND HUNDREDFOLD ANOINTING

LEVELS OF ANOINTING

THE ANOINTING IS costly and yet priceless. I know this may seem paradoxical, but it is very much true. The anointing is costly in that it may require much pain and suffering. This pain can be tangible, as in the loss of material possessions such as automobiles or homes and so forth. But there is no quantitative amount that can be attributed to the anointing to establish a price; therefore, it is priceless. For example, it is erroneous to say that an individual who has lost a car or house is more eligible for a hundredfold anointing than another individual who has lost his wife and child to a car accident and lives alone in his Beverly Hills mansion and drives a Mercedes-Benz. It is evident that there is an underlying cost that is not calculable but it is paid in full by the carriers of the anointing. Matthew states:

> And every one that hath forsaken houses, or brethren, or sisters, or father, or mother, or wife, or children, or

lands, for my name's sake, shall receive an hundredfold, and shall inherit everlasting life.
—Matthew 19:29

The anointing is priceless; and the carriers of it do not get
to bargain for, set a claim to, or have free access to it. God is
still the overseer of who is worthy of housing the anointing.
I believe every Christian is anointed; however, several scriptures indicate that there are different levels of anointing.

When God has destined you for an unusual anointing,
great trials, tribulations, pain, and suffering will precede
your possessing this hundredfold anointing. This anointing
will be revealed and released in stages such as thirtyfold, sixtyfold, and then a hundredfold.

While we all are a part of one body, which is Jesus Christ,
we all have different functions in that body. The hands, feet,
nose, eyes, and mouth all have different assignments. In
the natural, each part of the body has a certain amount of
strength that enables it to carry out its assigned function.
The muscles are uniquely designed and fashioned to fit its
particular task of the body. The apostle Paul was vivid in
1 Corinthians 12 when he used the analogy of the human
body to explain the working of the gifts of God by the same
Spirit. He went on to explain that there are various gifts
shared among the body of believers even as there are various
callings. God has given us the anointing that is needed to
function in those specified assigned areas. In essence, we are
all anointed to function in the body of Christ; and what
that function is will determine the level of our anointing.

Excelling from Glory to Glory

When God's hand is upon an individual for service, He does
not just move them from A to Z (thirtyfold to a hundredfold

anointing) overnight. Rather, a chosen vessel is progressively moved from glory to glory by God's orchestrated processing fire. Many potentially great men and women of God have had "spiritual miscarriages" because they wanted to move from getting saved one week to becoming a deliverance minister the next. The increasing reproach that is brought to Christianity by these sorts of things can be avoided when individuals are willing to be processed before they are promoted in the spiritual arena. Much of the elevation in the spiritual realm is shaped by some sort of processing (trials, tribulations, pain, and suffering), which God has ordained to catapult us to our destiny. This period will progressively move us into our specific calling from zero to thirtyfold to sixtyfold anointing and so forth. If we endure, it will eventually move us to the hundredfold anointing.

A chosen vessel is progressively moved from glory to glory by God's orchestrated processing fire.

Although every Christian has the potential to receive a hundredfold anointing, unfortunately this will not be an actual realization for everyone. Some will break down before they break through. An excellent example of this would be college hopefuls; entering college does not automatically denote graduation; the student must first complete every class and pass every test given by their instructors to qualify for graduation. As the student moves from class to class by successfully completing each level of his or her assignment, he or she becomes more skillful and knowledgeable. However, this still does not mean the student is capable or ready to operate in the fullness of his or her career. There is more knowledge to be attained in more advanced classes. A student at this stage can be classified as operating in 0 to 30 percent or even 30 to 90 percent of his or her ability. But that student still will not graduate and receive a degree until the end of the course when he or she has accomplished 100 percent of the requirements. Similarly those called by God (His chosen vessels) will not operate in the fullness of God's power until every class and test given by their Instructor (the Holy Ghost) is taken and the process is successfully completed. Only then will this person be proven to be a worthy candidate for a carrier of the hundredfold anointing.

A TASTE OF GOD'S GOODNESS

It is easy to misinterpret the operational capacity of the thirtyfold anointing as the ultimate level in God. While many boast that they are called as an apostle, prophet, evangelist, pastor, teacher, praise team leader, armor bearer, and so forth, they still fall short of operating in the hundredfold anointing. Yes the calling might be authentic; but of equal importance is the level of the "fold" in which they are operating (thirtyfold, sixtyfold, or hundredfold).

When we are operating in the hundredfold anointing, we are realizing our full God-given ability. However, to be satisfied to operate at the lower levels is an insult to God. It is tempting to settle for less than a hundredfold anointing because it will eliminate many classes from the school of hard knocks. You may be called as an apostle, prophet, or evangelist, etc.; but it does not mean that you are operating in 100 percent of the anointing God has for you. But at the same time it does not mean you are off track or out of God's timing.

You can operate in a thirtyfold or sixtyfold anointing and still be right on schedule with God's divine plans for you as long as you do not settle for what you have and your desire is to be used more of God. This type of hunger and drive will eventually lead you toward the hundredfold anointing and power that God has destined for your life. Always remember, God will not just take you there (to the hundredfold anointing) without testing, refining, maturing, and equipping you to be able to house this level of anointing. I am moved by the words of the great apostle Peter:

> But the God of all grace, who hath called us unto his eternal glory by Christ Jesus, after that ye have suffered a while, make you perfect, establish, strengthen, settle you.
>
> —1 PETER 5:10

Peter is inferring that God first calls us unto His eternal glory before sending us out to operate in His glory (power and anointing). This is not a one-way activity; when God calls us, we must subsequently answer the call in word, action, and deed. The reward for operating in the hundredfold anointing is eternal glory. Yet prior to the glory there is discomfort, for it is not until you have suffered awhile that the glory is revealed. Wow! That means after God calls us He processes us.

God in His wisdom compounds together the perfect formula (trials and tribulations) to progressively move us from thirtyfold to sixtyfold and then on to the hundredfold anointing (operating power) to carry out our assignments to their fullest. Although the application of these formulas can be uncomfortable and may be misconceived as the devil's doings, they are designed to bring the best out of us. It is essential to recognize the hand of God in every situation. The Bible tells us that all things work together for the good of those who are called by God (Rom. 8:28). The "sufferings of this present time are" going to result in an eternal glory (v. 18).

God in His wisdom compounds together
the perfect formula to progressively move
us from thirtyfold to sixtyfold and then
on to the hundredfold anointing.

While it is we (God's chosen vessels) who will be used as instruments of God's handiwork, we must be careful to give Him the glory. One of the easiest ways to fail is to become prideful and to elevate the created rather than the Creator (Rom. 1:25). The wisdom of the Book of Proverbs declares: "Pride goes before destruction, And a haughty spirit before a fall" (16:18, NKJV).

Too many leaders seem to be worshipping themselves rather than worshipping God. Rather than bringing glory to God, they are demanding they be worshipped. I would agree that the anointing that some are carrying is worthy of honor, but there is a thin line between honor and glory. While there is nothing wrong with serving the people of God, we have to be careful that we do not worship them as gods. Remember, Peter declared, "The God of all grace...called us to His eternal glory" (1 Pet. 5:10). His glory, not ours; His ways, not ours; and His wisdom, not ours. To operate in the hundredfold anointing, we must humble ourselves under the mighty hand of God (v. 6) and give Him all the glory.

One of the reasons God calls us first is so He can tutor us. God will allow us to go through His orchestrated mentoring fire not to destroy us but to make us perfect, established, strengthened, and then settled in the finishing anointing, which is the hundredfold anointing.

THE PRINCIPLE OF EXCELLENT THINGS

Several authors have devoted much study to understanding the anointing and spiritual gifting. Lori Wilke, a powerful woman of God, has written about it extensively and provides a clear thrust for such deliberations. Lori makes special mention of the various levels of anointing: the thirtyfold, sixtyfold and hundredfold anointing, in her dynamic book called *The Costly Anointing*. She maintains that there is a threefold truth which is known as "the principle of 'excellent things.' The word for 'excellent things' in Hebrew is *shalowsh*, which means" three or triple.[1] When applied to the anointing, we have a tri-phrase anointing, whereas an individual can go through three stages of spiritual enlightenment. The duration in each phrase differs from person to person; and in some cases it might be so short-lived that it is overlooked or too insignificant to be given any long-term attention. Nevertheless, research has proven that spiritual maturation is a process that evolves over time.

There are many scriptural examples that attest to the tri-fold anointing of God's chosen vessels. The biblical account given of Noah, for instance, contains elements of tri-level spiritual dimensions. Each believer undergoes three progressive spiritual experiences: justification, sanctification, and glorification. These three elements can also be seen in God's relationship with Noah. That is, Noah was justified in God's sight because God viewed him as a righteous man. Secondly, Noah was sanctified because he lived a holy and revered life before God and the people around him. Finally, Noah was glorified because of his obedience; God made him shine in the midst of those who had ridiculed and scorned him. While glory is the end result, it may be inferred that pain and trials accompany this glorification. The account of Noah's adventure with the ark has a wonderful ending, even though there are parts of the narrative that are very troublesome. Noah's glory came with a price: the price of rejection, loneliness, and embarrassment. The people in Noah's neighborhood did not support him but rather mocked and laughed at him. When embodying the hundredfold anointing, we have to be prepared to sail through the many snares of the enemy.

Old Testament literature has much to say about the anointing; and although coded for the most part, there are still some explicit examples of the tri-fold anointing. David was anointed three times, which symbolized the thirtyfold, sixtyfold, and the hundredfold anointing. David was first anointed by Samuel the prophet in his father's house (1 Sam. 16:13), which represented his thirtyfold anointing. Later he was anointed king over Judah (2 Sam. 2:4), which represented his sixtyfold anointing. The third anointing was as king over Israel (5:3), which represented his hundredfold anointing. Some would think that one anointing by the prophet Samuel should have been all it took for David to move immediately into his kingship. Yet, there was still more training for him to undergo and other levels to attain.

Those who will harness a hundredfold anointing will receive it in stages—thirtyfold, sixtyfold, and finally hundredfold. This harnessing requires the receiver to endure God's orchestrated mentoring fire, which is intended to transport them to higher and higher heights in the anointing. God progressively moves in threefold dimensions; for instance, in the tabernacle and the temple there were the outer court, the inner court, and the holy of holies. The called by God may move through similar dimensions.

It can be at a steady pace or the progression can fluctuate, depending on the individual and the calling. Often God moves us progressively from one level to another as we meet His requirements of each level. No matter how great you become or how qualified, how strong, or how intellectual you think you are, God will not take you directly into your destiny. Progressively you will arrive at a state of excellence, maturity, strength, wisdom, and power.

THIRTYFOLD ANOINTING (OUTER COURT ANOINTING)

The thirtyfold anointing is a preparatory anointing; what I call a starter's anointing. It does not matter whether you are called as an apostle, prophet, pastor, evangelist, teacher, bishop, elder, praise team leader, prayer warrior, or even a pope; all Christians must pass through a thirtyfold anointing in route to the sixtyfold anointing. The danger of trying to bypass this stage is that you will miss out on the spiritual foundation that God establishes at this level that is so vital to the building and strength of your ministry. Hence, when trials surface that are normally encountered in the sixty-fold realm, many leaders crumble because they did not go through the prior thirtyfold anointing requirements needed before they advanced. I believe on this thirtyfold level is where God removes the unnecessary stuff in our lives, cleans up the clutter, and begins to work on us so that we would be equipped to move on to deeper work. There are leaders occupying the chief seats in Christian arenas who have not gone through this spiritual spring-cleaning in their personal lives and yet are launching spiritual clean-up campaigns in their neighbors' lives. God is calling such persons back to the thirtyfold anointing level so that they can be effective and fully prepared to lead and lead by example.

The outer court anointing is important to the maturation of the saints. During your processing at the thirtyfold level of anointing, you become more sensitive to the movement and operation of the Spirit. Your ability to hear, discern, understand, digest, and apply the Word of God to your life is heightened and sharpened. I believe that there is much seeking in this preparatory stage, with the Word of God forming the basis of the search for deeper spiritual enlightenment. So it is then, at this stage, that the individual is grounded in the Word of God and receives a solid spiritual foundation for personal growth. Because the Word is Jesus and Jesus is the Word (John 1:1), having daily encounters with the Word on this thirtyfold level is having daily encounters with Jesus Christ. A personal relationship with Jesus Christ is developed on this level. God wants to saturate our spirit and soul (will, mind, and emotions) with His Word. After being saturated with the Word and truly believing it, revelation and manifestation will take place.

The call, the power, and the anointing of God for your life starts to manifest at the thirtyfold level. Remember, God will only use humble, available, teachable, and willing vessels. Those who are disobedient and arrogant will choke the anointing, which will result in an abortion of their assignment. It is important to be a willing and yielded vessel, pliable enough for God to transform you into His chosen vessel created to duplicate His character and power in the earth. This thirtyfold, preparatory anointing is the foundation anointing the individual (vessel of God) will be built upon. The mere fact that God has chosen you indicates that you have what it takes to do the job. The enemy is aware of your potential and will do all in his power to prevent you from successfully fulfilling God's will.

During the thirtyfold season you must be careful of your surroundings. The anointing is delicate and must be carefully preserved. In this thirtyfold period how you respond to what you see, hear, know, and experience will determine your promotion to the sixtyfold anointing. This is the beginning of the faith journey for the called, for no longer will the anointed walk by sight. From here on in the journey is based on faith to believe beyond what has been scientifically proven or what is categorized as possible. This is a place of blind trust where God has the upper hand and we must follow. He takes us to the problem and expects us to trust Him to bring us safely through. In some ways we are like little children, following our Father with the conviction that He knows what's best for us; just as an earthly father is there for his child, God will hold our hands to subside our fear and provide for our needs. In the thirtyfold, preparatory anointing is where we learn how to follow Jesus even when we can't trace Him.

Thirty is the number of maturity. Remember, Jesus did not begin His ministry until the age of thirty, even though He was called from the foundation of the world. God had placed His seal upon the Christ child to be the Savior of the world; but this was materialized at the right time of maturation. The fact still remains that once we are operating in a human flesh there is a process that we all must go through. Once the Word (Jesus) became wrapped in human flesh, He became subject to a progressive spiritual operation. There is not much written about His childhood except for the little we glean in the Gospel of Luke about Jesus' journey to Jerusalem at the age of twelve (2:42) and the ending of this narrative stating: "And Jesus increased in wisdom and stature, and in favour with God and man" (v. 52). This gives a clear indication that there was progressive maturity that took place in His life. Therefore, we can surmise that we too will experience progression, both in the physical and spiritual realms.

The entry level of the anointing (thirtyfold) is important to the body of Christ. Those at the hundredfold level can enjoy such anointing because of having been through this entry level of the thirtyfold anointing. Prior to reaching the hundredfold anointing, the carrier would have undergone many struggles and mistakes and had many questions for God. Hence, the thirtyfold anointing is essential in that it helps bring us to a place of maturity, not just in our actions, attitudes, and behavior; but more importantly in our understanding, acceptance, and operation in our calling and anointing

By the time a person passes through the thirtyfold realm, they would have been settled in the kingdom, knowing their gifting and what they are called to do. The apostle Paul declared: "Let every man abide in the same calling wherein he was called" (1 Cor. 7:20). You should have grown in spiritual maturity by the time you come into the sixtyfold anointing; you should know whether you are called by God to be a prophet or an usher. It is expedient that we do not dismiss the necessary things gained at the entry level. We do not want to become a hindrance and mockery to the kingdom because of our ignorance and immaturity.

Although there is power and glory involved at this thirtyfold level, there is still much to learn, experience, and endure before graduating. Don't become like so many who have gotten stuck at this level. God has given you what you need to successfully complete each assignment at each level. Once you progress deeper and to more challenging assignments, the need to flow in a greater anointing will be evident.

The thirtyfold anointing can be likened unto the outer court. The outer court in the tabernacle of Moses was a place of sacrifice; an animal had to be put to death and sacrificed on the brazen altar, also called the altar of sacrifice. The Hebrew root word for *altar* means to slay or slaughter. At this thirtyfold level we too must experience the altar of sacrifice by putting our flesh to death. This is necessary before we can enter into His presence, which is in the greater inner court (the sixtyfold anointing). Also in the outer court was the bronze laver (basin) that was filled with water so that the priest could wash his hands and feet before entering into God's presence. During this thirtyfold realm, not only will our flesh be put to death but we will also be washed and cleansed by the Word of God.

God has intended for many to operate in the unusual hundredfold anointing; but after preaching, prophesying, singing, and so forth, under the thirtyfold anointing of power and glory, many have become complacent and comfortable at this entry level, not willing or wanting to experience the trials of suffering and pain necessary to propel them into a greater level of God's power. Why are we settling for mediocrity or entry level to anything when there are higher heights to achieve? I firmly believe that you—yes you—reading this book are a part of the remnant God has ordained to "press toward the mark for the prize [hundredfold anointing] of the high calling of God in Christ Jesus" (Phil. 3:14).

The question still stands: "Are you willing to pay the price to move from the thirtyfold to sixtyfold anointing?" It's amazing that you can find church folks who have been toiling in the ministry for ten, twenty, or thirty years and are still drinking spiritual milk that is for new babes in Christ (Heb. 5:13). Then there are those who wear big titles across their chests or pope hats yet are content with being used at the thirtyfold level despite the fact that the feasibility of launching out into the deep and destroying the enemies' vices and strongholds hinges upon moving in the power and grace of a hundredfold anointing. The sad part about this is that some folks don't desire to press on for a greater anointing and yet spend their time fighting with and hating those who have the desire and are pressing toward the mark.

The anointing is for the entire body of Christ; and as such the levels are obtainable by all who will seek it. However, as often is the case, everybody wants the glory but nobody wants to have a story behind the glory. Every great man or woman has a story behind their glory. Even Jesus was not exempt. Are you willing to pay the price? It comes with much pain and suffering; but there is nothing that can be compared to the glory received once you endure to the end.

Sixtyfold Anointing (Inner Court Anointing)

The experiences gained during the thirtyfold anointing usher the called of God into a deeper spiritual thrust called the sixtyfold anointing. The vessel should at this time be well able to house a greater anointing for his or her assignment in the kingdom. At this level of maturity, the individual will begin to look away from self and develop a keen interest and concern for the people and work of God. The need to promote a personal agenda is eradicated to the extent that God's will has become the sole purpose of ministry. At this level the Christian (the chosen) portrays similar qualities to the character of Jesus Christ, exemplifying love, commitment, faithfulness, and integrity. This is an anointing that is recognized instantly, for the ground is fertile and cultivated in such a way that "you will know them by their fruits" (Matt. 7:16, NKJV).

There is a notable difference between the thirtyfold, sixtyfold, and hundredfold anointing. For instance, the thirtyfold to sixtyfold anointing is the "alpha" anointing (beginning, preparatory) while the hundredfold is the "omega" (finishing) anointing. No matter what your calling is, you will progressively move from glory (thirtyfold level) to glory (sixtyfold level) to glory (hundredfold level) of God's glory, power, and anointing for your specific calling. Hence, there is no need to be envious of another's disposition of gifts and anointing. Even if two persons are called to the same office but one advances faster than the other and hence operates at a higher level, it does not mean that the other would not eventually achieve the hundredfold anointing. The ones who endure the testing will be those who God will move from thirtyfold to sixtyfold and eventually to the hundredfold anointing. Remember, it's "not by might, nor by power, but by my spirit, saith the LORD of hosts" (Zech. 4:6). God's power, anointing, and favor will enable us to operate in the fullness of our callings.

Those who have made it to this level should be well tuned for God to play like an instrument for the purpose of advancing the kingdom. Many individuals, as was mentioned earlier, become complacent at the thirtyfold level, hence forfeiting the opportunity for growth needed to effectively be played as instruments by God. It would sound like an organ being played only in the minor keys. Many that have been chosen by God have failed to realize their full potential; therefore, the major keys have not yet been touched (the greater anointing).

Fear of reaching out into the spiritual realm can rob us of the joy of living fully for God. There is more joy in the inner court; we just need to step out of the outer court and transition into the sixtyfold anointing. It is in the inner court where we become more in tune with the heart of God. It is here that we realize that God is in control and that "the weapons of our warfare are not carnal, but mighty through God to the pulling down of strong holds" (2 Cor. 10:4). The chosen of God are now strengthened to run with firmer steps knowing full well that it is God who enables the great exploits to take place.

The sixtyfold is a power-packed anointing. When one operates in the spirit with this weight of glory, his or her gifting (preaching, prophesying, teaching, singing, or praying, etc.) becomes much easier, smoother, and more powerful. Whatever was difficult to do at the thirtyfold level now becomes natural and armed with competence and skill. At the thirtyfold level, for instance, showing up at church meetings was a pain because you knew every idea you presented would be rejected; so you made a conscious effort to show up late or hoped to get a flat tire on the way so you wouldn't have to show up at all. Your outlook is different once you hit the sixtyfold anointing; you turn up for meetings on time with typewritten proposals and a smile that says, "So what if you shut down my ideas. God will just open another door since it is His proposal and not mine." The power that goes with the sixtyfold anointing continuously reminds the carrier to rejoice in tribulation and bless those from whom persecution arises. We can only rejoice when we are confident that the assignment we are on has been appointed with a failure-proof anointing to carry out the Master's task successfully.

The sixtyfold anointing can be likened unto the inner court in the tabernacle of Moses where you would find the table of shewbread (bread of the presence). This symbolizes fellowship and communion with God. In this sixtyfold realm is where the anointed will experience unusual encounters with the presence of God like he or she never experienced before. Also during this time as you feast on the Word of God (the shewbread), revelation such as you never experienced before will spring forth.

Another awesome masterpiece that was found in the inner court was the golden candlestick (lampstand), which symbolizes the constant working of the Holy Spirit in our lives. During this sixtyfold (inner court) realm, you will experience the Holy Spirit's presence so strong that there will be a turning in your belly; Jesus called this "rivers of living water" (John 7:38). Wow! The sixtyfold anointing is great; but you can't stop there. God's got much more in store for you.

Finally in the inner court was found the altar of incense, which represented the prayers of the believers. On this level your prayer life will shift to another dimension and the anointing to intercede on behalf of others will breathe instant results as your prayers will stay in the presence of God. During the sixtyfold stage you will receive much insight and revelation from God to function and operate skillfully in your calling.

But there is more to go through before you get to the final (hundredfold) glory, power, and anointing. The price to attain this level is extremely high; an attempt to reach this final level might cause you to feel as if you are losing your mind, not to mention that your very life might be endangered because of the intensity of the troubles and trials you must pass through. If you are willing to risk all and reach it, the power and glory afforded to you is so astronomical; it will by far outweigh any trials you went through to get there. This hundredfold anointing is the finest and highest level that one can reach in their calling; you would then be operating at 100 percent of what God has intended for your life. You and I know that at every level there are devils; but I believe at this final level legions of them exist. Hence, this level is not for the feeble in heart but for the giants of the faith. Are you willing to pay the price?

The term *faith* must be emphasized here because the battle is not ours, it belongs to God, and our role is to simply trust Him. The following scriptures attest to this:

> Ye are of God, little children, and have overcome them: because greater is he that is in you, than he that is in the world.
>
> —1 JOHN 4:4

> When the enemy shall come in like a flood, the Spirit of the LORD shall lift up a standard against him.
>
> —ISAIAH 59:19

> Not by might, nor by power, but by my Spirit, saith the LORD of hosts.
>
> —ZECHARIAH 4:6

In each of these findings, the authority lies outside of the vessel; it is the One who calls the vessel that ensures the success. This is why Moses, a servant of God, who perhaps was one of the greatest leaders on earth, told the Lord that He needed the presence of God to go with him (Exod. 33:15). The biggest trick of Satan today is to influence the called of God into believing that we are operating in our own strength. Many have fallen for this trick and are suffering the consequences. We are mere vessels being used for God's glory, and it is only through Jesus Christ that we are able to do all things; hence the praise belongs to God.

To move into the hundredfold realm requires you to move from being just a soldier to becoming a warrior. The difference between a soldier and a warrior is that soldiers sometimes quit, retreat, surrender, or turn back when the battle gets too hot; but a warrior will stare the enemy in the face and with courage and determination fight unto death even when wounded and outnumbered. The warrior is not distracted by the threats, traps, or attacks from the opponents; for it is in these times that true warriors optimize full potential and rise to the occasion. My comrades, if you are going to make it to that destined place and operate in 100 percent of your calling, you've got to develop the spirit of a warrior. The spirit of a warrior will take you through your final testing for the greater; you must be determined not to settle for 10, 20, 30, 40, 50, 60, 70, 80, or even 99 percent of your spiritual inheritance. The goal is to reach the hundredfold anointing; and may I remind you that everything you need is there—increase, overflow, deliverance and more than enough joy, peace, happiness, and so forth.

No matter how close you are to 100 percent of God's plans, purposes, and power for your life, your cry must still be that 99 1/2 just won't do. Declare three times into the atmosphere until hell gets the message: "I am going for the greater! I am going for the greater! I am going for the greater hundredfold anointing!" Amen.

BETWEEN THE SIXTYFOLD AND
HUNDREDFOLD ANOINTING

God's desire is for us to fully achieve and operate in the hundredfold anointing. There is a great price to be paid to move from thirtyfold to sixtyfold and then to the hundredfold anointing. We have to go through a period of testing. Jesus said, "If any man will come after me, let him deny himself, and take up his cross daily, and follow me" (Luke 9:23). Promotion comes with a price. Are you willing to pay that price? On your way to the hundredfold anointing God will allow you to experience great and sore troubles. The journey to the hundredfold anointing will cause you great pain and suffering.

On your way up the ladder, climbing the steps of spiritual greatness, you must develop a spirit of praise and worship; this will sustain you during the journey. God is at the top rooting (cheering) for you to excel. You only have to look up; the hundredfold anointing is closer than you think. The temptation to settle for less is real; but don't give in. While the sixtyfold anointing is precious, you still need an additional fortyfold power, glory, and anointing to maximize your spiritual potential.

My friend, the sad news is that forty is the number of testing. Are you willing to pay the price? Ervin N. Hershberger in his book *Seeing Christ in the Tabernacle*, claims: "Forty is the number of testing and probation."[2] (See Luke 4:2.) Just as forty is the number of testing, I believe the fortyfold between the sixtyfold and hundredfold anointing is also a time of testing. This is the time when God will allow the enemy, along with his entourage, access to attack you in every area of your life whether marital, personal, financial, mental, physical, or spiritual. Unbeknownst to your attackers, haters, and rivalries, God will use these fiery trials to build, develop, equip, and qualify you for the greater (hundredfold) of God's operating power. Moreover, I believe this period of testing, although rigorous, is vital to God's chosen vessels. There is much to be gained through enduring this period.

Moving from the sixtyfold to the hundredfold anointing may be very costly; sometimes having to risk everything you presently have or hope to gain. In order for God to increase our greatness, we must pass through the trials that have been orchestrated by Him (God).

HUNDREDFOLD ANOINTING (THE HOLY OF HOLIES)

Operating in the hundredfold anointing simply means that the individual is functioning in 100 percent wisdom, glory, power, and anointing that are necessary to succeed in his or her ministry or purpose. Once the hundredfold anointing is obtained, it allows the carrier to operate in the holy of holies. The holy of holies is a place of unlimited possibilities; it is where the Divine (God) empowers humanity to operate in supernatural ways.

In the holy of holies is where you would find the ark of the covenant. The ark was a symbol of the presence and power of God. The hundredfold realm is where you would experience the presence and power of God in its fullness. Also within the ark was a golden pot of manna symbolizing God's supernatural provision. On this hundredfold level you will truly know God as Jehovah Jireh, your supernatural Provider. Because of the level of power and anointing you would be packing on this level, God will supernaturally protect and provide for you. The enemy will come in like a flood, but on this level ex nihilo (out of nothing) God will create for His chosen.

Also within the ark was Aaron's rod that budded, symbolizing God openly making a difference between His chosen and those who are just carrying a name and have no power. Numbers chapters 16 and 17 tell how Aaron's rod came about. Korah and his entourage rose up against Moses and Aaron declaring that they were anointed by God as well. Swiftly God moved against Korah and his crew by opening the earth and allowing them to be swallowed. God then commanded Moses to take a rod from the children of Israel each according to the house of their fathers, twelve rods. He told them to write Aaron's name upon the rod of Levi and then to lay them all in the tabernacle of the congregation before the testimony. He said that the man whose rod blossomed would be the one He had chosen. When they went to check them the next day, it was discovered that Aaron's rod had blossomed. Here's what the Bible says:

> And it came to pass, that on the morrow Moses went into the tabernacle of witness; and, behold, the rod of Aaron for the house of Levi was budded, and brought forth buds, and bloomed blossoms, and yielded almonds…And the LORD said unto Moses, Bring Aaron's rod again before the testimony, to be kept for a token against the rebels; and thou shalt quite take away their murmurings from me, that they die not.
> —NUMBERS 17:8, 10

Thus God openly declared to Israel that Aaron was His choice and this ended the murmuring among the people.

On this level of favor, power, and anointing, God will make plain those carrying His name; it will be undeniable. The rebels will be silenced because of the incredible manifestation of the power of God in your life. You'd better get ready; God is about to make music out of your life. What was difficult to accomplish before will now happen supernaturally on this hundredfold level. Are you willing to pay the price?

Entering into this realm of anointing and power places you into the vein and center of God's ultimate will for your life. Because you have reached your destined place, you can never let your guard down. Remember, the enemy has you on his hit list as a most wanted.

To maintain this level of anointing and power, it is a must that you stay in the presence of God. There is no time for idleness. One of the most powerful weapons of Satan against those who have reached this level of anointing is called "busyness." The people of God are just too busy; they are even too busy to recognize the decay in their immediate environment. On this level you must use your time wisely. Stay in the presence of the Lord and be guided by God's mandate; because in a moment when you think not, the debris of life might be thrown in your direction. Take cover and find refuge in the shadow of the Almighty.

When a meteorologist wants to study a hurricane to determine the magnitude and strength of it, they often fly a weather plane into the eye of the storm. In a similar vein, the carriers of the hundredfold anointing will have the ability through the Spirit of God to know the direction, magnitude, and strength of the enemy; therefore, being equipped for this type of warfare because of past experiences and spiritual insight, they will overcome the adversary every time. The apostle Paul said in Romans 8:37: "In all these things we are more than conquerors through him that loved us." Remember, we, God's warriors, are more than conquerors.

Because of the vicious attacks of the enemy, not many

arrive at this level of power and anointing. This dimension of power and glory is also a place of loneliness and surprises, such as family, friends, and so forth walking away from you, betraying you, and even seeking to assassinate you. The price of this powerful anointing is costly. How bad do you want it? Do you want it bad enough to endure whatever the enemy sends your way?

Because of your determination, the devil, along with his cohorts, will use every trick in the book to bring you to a standstill. But you must tell yourself, "I have come too far to turn back now." The mega that's ahead of you, my friend, is worth it; and those who oppose you will see and know that who God blesses no man can curse. The prophet Balaam said to Balak in Numbers 23:20, "Behold, I have received commandment to bless: and he hath blessed; and I cannot reverse it."

The torture of the enemy doesn't feel good; in fact, it is at these moments when feelings of loneliness and rejection and spiritual suicide (throwing in the towel) are most prevalent. Yet, it is these adverse conditions that your giftings are sharpened, your mind is refined, your strength is renewed, and your anointing increases. The remnant operating in this vein of God's glory and power will be relentless; they will tear down Satan's kingdom and bring deliverance to God's people.

When you are in the perfect will of God, operating in the hundredfold of your calling, storms have very little or no effect on you; you feel invincible and unstoppable. The hundredfold anointing is a storm-calming, water-walking, winds-behaving, sea-settling, earthshaking, paradigm-shifting, and yoke-destroying anointing.

The Bible declares:

> From the days of John the Baptist until now the kingdom of heaven suffereth violence, and the violent take it by force.
>
> —MATTHEW 11:12

The chosen vessels of God are now going where no man has gone before, breaking through barriers, leaping over walls, tearing down satanic strongholds, and accomplishing that which man said was impossible. This hundredfold anointing (operating in the fullness of what God has called you into) is a terror to Satan's kingdom. The hundredfold anointing will give you the ability to do God's will in the midst of tumult, opposition, difficulties, and danger. Serious times require the people of God to operate in a higher level of anointing. I truly believe that God has chosen you for such a time as this. Hang in there; the best is yet to come!

The authority received at the hundredfold realm births a level of spiritual boldness that casts away all fears. Persons at this realm will charge into demonic territories to set the captive free and while there challenge any demon or devil to stop them.

While the anointing of God is for the people of God, there is much value in operating in the fullness of God (the hundredfold anointing). God wants to pour out His Spirit upon all flesh so that we can achieve the greater works of Jesus Christ (Acts 2:17); but it comes with a price. Once we are willing to pay the price, we can live victorious lives through the eminent power of God. It is imperative that those called of God operate in the hundredfold realm. The hundredfold anointing is a threefold anointing; and as the great King Solomon declares, "A threefold cord is not quickly broken" (Eccles. 4:12).

Indeed, the tedious and harsh process that accompanies

this anointing is great but it will give the endurance needed to fully equip and mature the saints to handle their assignments. The men and women whom God is raising up in this hour will not be shaken or detoured; they will "be steadfast, immovable, always abounding in the work of the Lord" (1 Cor. 15:58). Are you willing to pay the price?

Chapter Five

THE AFTEREFFECT

The Aftereffect Defined

W<small>E TREASURE THOSE</small> moments in life that bring us joy and often file such events away in our memory banks; but seldom do we hold dear and unwrap the lessons that come from undesirable occurrences. In both experiences there is what I refer to as an aftereffect, which once tapped into can hold great benefits for the rest of life's journey. Although commonly used, the word *after* is defined by Webster's as "a result of, in the rear, next or later." The word *after* tells us of something that follows something else. A good example would be the old proverb, what goes up, must come down; something goes up but it does not stay there, the same thing that goes up must come down. Thus the coming down will be considered the aftereffect. The word *effect* according to Webster's is defined as "something that inevitably follows an antecedent (as a cause or agent)." Hence, it is the general consensus of this chapter that every human experience will leave a good, bad, negative, or positive effect upon us, which ultimately can *affect* (to produce an effect or change in, to impress the mind or move the feelings) our future.

God never promised that we will have sunshine every day,

but He knew that there would be times of discouragement. Hence, He promised to work the bad times out for the good. Nevertheless, we have free will and can choose to trust God to work it out or can be disgruntled about the mountains in our pathway.

The story is told about a boy who wanted to be a heavyweight champion like his dad. One day the young lad told his father about his desire to lift weights. The dad immediately took him to the gym, showed him the equipment, and asked, "Are you sure you want to lift weights?" The boy, filled with excitement, blurted out, "Yes sir! Dad will you coach me?" The father, filled with pride, took his son to the backyard of the gym, showed him a dilapidated freezer, and told him to push. The boy looked at his father with utter confusion; then going to the freezer, he began pushing. He became more and more frustrated as he pushed and pushed but could not move the freezer. The father sat calmly watching from a distance. Minutes later the boy screamed, "Dad, this doesn't make sense! I want to be a heavyweight champion not a garbage collector!" The boy pouted all the way home. When he had calmed down, the boy said, "Dad, you knew I could never move that freezer, so why did you give me such a difficult task?" The father replied, "I never told you to move the freezer. I told you to push it. The pushing would build muscles and strengthen your back."

The assignment God has given you requires spiritual maturity and strength; therefore, in the pushing, even when nothing seems to be moving or making sense, spiritual power is birthed (character, integrity, faithfulness, commitment, etc.). So push on regardless.

There are emotional aftereffects to each trial one suffers. For instance, a divorcee can experience the aftereffects of anger, bitterness, hatred, and so forth. Likewise, those who have lost a job, house, car, money, friendship, and so forth are all left with the emotional aftereffects; they may feel betrayed, useless, slandered, hurt, mistreated, or disappointed. These feelings can cause dangerous reactions if allowed to develop into bitterness. A happy ending does not always mean a happy person. Some folks after suffering remain bitter, regardless of the aftermath. A bitter person is a dangerous person and can never be trusted with kingdom authority (power, anointing, influence, and favor). When the outcome of experiences leaves someone bitter, they can easily resent those around them and even go as far as resenting God. A person who embraces the better, on the other hand, accepts the pains of yesterday and rejoices in the joys of today. For the person who decides to become better rather than bitter, past hurts and horrible experiences are seen as stepping stones to greatness. We must strive to get better and not bitter through the trials of life.

As I travel through this Christian journey, I discover that God uses betrayal, denial, abandonment, rejection, opposition, slander, mistreatment, disappointment, and so forth as tools to prepare us for His ultimate purpose. However, I must concede that when faced with such adverse conditions, there is the temptation to become bitter; and those called by God are not exempt from such temptation. When you are attacked, abused, mistreated, and mishandled by those you felt were on your side (yes, even those church folks who God has given you to minister to), it is very important that you guard your heart. You have too much to lose; God is depending on you.

You might be saying right now, "Man of God, if I've got too much to lose and God is counting on me, then why is He allowing me to go through all of this?" For the same reason He allowed His only begotten Son to go through all of the rejection, betrayal, pain and crucifixion; so that He could give Him the power for the hour (assignment). God is searching for some people who would be like Timex: It takes a licking and keeps on ticking (functioning as purposed).

Notice that in spite of what Jesus went through and the betrayal of those who caused His pain and suffering, He never became bitter. In fact His cry was "Father, forgive them; for they know not what they do" (Luke 23:34). This is the cry that God is listening for from His chosen vessels after their processing. No matter who hurt you, wronged you, or tried to destroy you, you must be able to respond to them in the spirit of power and love. Joseph said unto his brothers who hated him and had sold him as a slave: "You meant evil against me; but God meant it for good, in order to bring it about as it is this day, to save (deliver) many people alive" (Gen. 50:20, NKJV). In other words, Joseph was saying unto them, "God worked it out; I was processed for your deliverance."

If you are being processed for the deliverance of God's people, how then can you come out of the fire bitter instead of better and angry with those you have to now minister to and still expect God to anoint you? My comrade, the prerequisite for this powerful anointing (hundredfold anointing) is that after you have been tried in the fire, you must come out as pure gold with no impurities (bitterness, hatred, anger, resentment, and so forth). Remember, the power released by God upon your life is fully determined by the aftereffect of your process: bitter or better. No matter what happens, God is still in control.

> The power released by God upon your
> life is fully determined by the aftereffect
> of your process: bitter or better.

The prophet Isaiah said, "In the year that King Uzziah died I saw also the LORD sitting upon a throne, high and lifted up, and his train filled the temple." What Isaiah was saying here is that it was not until his Uncle Uzziah died that he experienced a mighty move of God in his life. God's man or God's woman, it is not until the *you* on the outside dies that the *you* on the inside will experience God in a real way. I don't know about you, but I am ready to experience the glory; and my flesh must die.

During the refining process, God will use anyone or any measures He chooses (spouse, friends, neighbors, believers, etc.) as stimuli to get us to a greater anointing. God knows exactly what you are able to bear and will not exhaust your abilities. Don't be dismayed, God sees your struggles and He is monitoring your encounters. Stop getting all upset and discouraged when the fiery darts come your way; God is in control. The author of the Book of Job puts it best when he declared: "But he knoweth the way that I take: when he hath tried me, I shall come forth as gold" (Job 23:10).

> During the refining process, God will use
> anyone or any measures He chooses as
> stimuli to get us to a greater anointing.

What you are going through now is intended to help get you to the place where you are destined to be in the near future. God knows the path you are on, and it is His intention that the carriers of this power-packed hundredfold anointing go through rigorous training to be well-rounded and equipped as a skilled warrior. You can choose to rejoice because of the promise and embrace the process or reject the process and forfeit the promise.

Many have passed through God's orchestrated mentoring fire and come out bitter—bitter with those whom God used as mentoring tools, bitter with God's people, and even bitter with the church. Hence they were not able to embrace all the hidden blessings that God had stored in the processing and therefore cannot be a carrier of the glory. Without the proper training and molding (development), an individual's spiritual condition will disqualify him or her for their God-ordained assignment. My friend, God expects us to endure and rejoice as we go through trials; it is a display of trust and confidence in our Savior.

Your Attitude Determines Your Altitude

What do you do when people that have scandalized your name, betrayed you, belittled you, or borrowed your money and wouldn't pay it back or people you have gone out on a limb for, you would have given up sleep and maybe even your very own life for come knocking at your door? Indeed, there will be an aftereffect from such experiences but the question to ask is will it make you bitter or better? The way you respond in situations can determine how far you go on the spirituality spectrum. God is desirous of persons who can take hardships and still stand. Bitterness, anger, frustration, hatred, and resentfulness only eat away at the promises of God. But the "better," which is love, joy, and forgiveness, feeds the promises of God, causing them to grow, expand,

and enlarge in your life. Often it is the people that have put us through hell on the way to greatness that we have to serve, and God requires this service to be in genuine love. The fiery furnace is only to qualify us for the promotion and condition us for the promise. You will confess one day that if it had not been for the things you have suffered, you would not have been as strong as you are now. Don't be bitter; rather let God use you to be a blessing to the world, even to your opponents. This is the true mark of maturity, and it is the gateway to the hundredfold anointing.

God's anointing and power will only rest upon the humble, meek, and prudent. The Bible declares that the humble child tastes the grace of God. Thus, it is in humility that we gladly turn and give the other cheek to those who strike us on the right cheek (Matt. 5:39). Too often we act in arrogance and seek revenge on those who have wronged us. This is what I call a bitter aftereffect. Reactions like this will cause you to forfeit the promises of God concerning you. God has not called us to get even with evildoers. The true vessels of God will not use the power, favor, and blessings of God to repay those who oppose them. Rather, God's chosen vessels will react in an unusual way when mistreated or mishandled. The joy of the Lord will cause them to rise above the status quo of "tit for tat" (if you hit me, I will hit you back) to embrace an attitude of blessing for cursing and love for hate. While our human nature might long for and subscribe to the vengeful, bitter aftereffect of fighting fire with fire, total submission to the will of God forces us to accept the bitterness of any situation and respond with a godly reaction of love, long-suffering, and forgiveness.

The power of forgiveness must be operational, especially in those who have been through the fiery furnace and want to be revealed as pure gold. The goldsmith places the gold in the fire until all of its impurities are gone. Like the gold-smith, God's plan is to keep us in the fire until all of the impurities are burnt out. The purification process is a very difficult one to bear and may lead many desiring to come out of the fire prematurely. My friend, a premature exit will only prolong the process because the goldsmith will need to reset the fire and place you back in the flames. Even if by some chance you are allowed to go on display in a prema-ture state, the results can be disappointing; for even as the audience often has an eye for fine jewelry and will know immediately the real from the fake, so will it be for that person who does not complete the process of being in the fire. Hence, the fire is necessary; and it is unfair for the gold to be upset, angry, and revengeful toward the fire, because it is the fire that gives it its true value. There are some people who are ordained to bombard your life to produce a kind of fire to bring you to perfection so that you will qualify for the greater. So, in the midst of the vicious attacks, back-biting, scandals, lies, and so forth, God still expects you to love, cherish, care, bless, and pray for those who tried to annihilate you.

Godly reaction toward those who have hurt you, opposed you, and caused you many sleepless nights is essential for those who will be carriers of this hundredfold anointing. Remember, it is your past that equips you for your future. Will the aftereffect of what you have been through be bitter or better? Edmund Burke once said, "He who wrestles with us, strengthens our nerves and sharpens our skills. Our antagonist is our helper."[1] I would go on to say that when weighed in the balance, our enemies are more of an asset to our future than our friends. For the trials, tribulations, and the pressures of life are what turn you inside out revealing the you that's on the inside. This is the *you* that God has ordained and who the world has never seen—changed, processed, and ready for the promise.

It's like an orange; what is the true value of an orange? Is it the outward appearance or is it what's on the inside of the orange that gives it its true value? The orange is not purchased because of the way it looks on the outside but because of the substance on the inside, its juice. But before you get to the juice you must disfigure the orange either by using a knife to peel the skin or to cut the orange in half, or by a juicer—the perfect method of extracting the juice from the orange. Using any of these means will leave the orange totally disfigured. Neither the knife nor the juicer is to blame for disfiguring the orange; the true blame goes to the one who purchased the orange and desired the juice. And can the orange really blame the one who bought it? The aftereffect can either be bitter or better.

God purchased us.

> What! Know ye not that your body is the temple of the Holy Ghost which is in you, which ye have of God, and ye are not your own? For ye are bought with a price: therefore glorify God in your body, and in your spirit, which are God's.
> —1 Corinthians 6:19–20

The apostle Paul is plainly saying here that our bodies are the place where God's Spirit (the juice, anointing) dwells and that we were bought by Him (God) for a price (shedding of Jesus' precious blood). So therefore, if we are bought by Him and are owned by Him, He has the rights to do anything He wants and to use anybody He chooses as instruments to extract His juice (anointing) out of us. The instruments (those whom God chooses to use) are not to be blamed. Nor can God be blamed. So at the end of the day, the only thing to blame is purpose; And purpose is the reason for you being here.

Rejoicing in Suffering

The process we go through for the anointing is for the most part strenuous, difficult, and challenging; but if we allow God to have His way, we will come out complete. James, the leader of the early church, declares:

> My brethren, count it all joy when ye fall into divers temptations; Knowing this, that the trying of your faith worketh patience. But let patience have her perfect work, that ye may be perfect and entire, wanting nothing.
>
> —James 1:2–4

James is saying that when we go through trials and tribulations our response should be one of rejoicing as opposed to the negative aftereffect of bitterness that is often displayed. These trials are designed to enhance our lives, increase our faith, and bring us to perfection. In the natural, in order to know the durability of any product it must first be tested; and so it is in the spiritual, the testing of our faith determines our ability to carry out the assignment God has given us. These trials are not designed to make us mean-spirited or resentful but rather to bring spiritual stability and maturity.

The most pressing question then is how can we find pleasure in suffering? The answer to questions like this is found in the Book of Psalms. In Psalm 23 David describes the Lord as a Shepherd who meets the sheep's every need. This Shepherd is so acquainted with and trusted by the sheep that even in the face of danger (death) the sheep have no fear. I do believe that most of our anxieties are created out of a lack of trust in our Shepherd. We react to the trials of life like people without hope or sheep without a Shepherd. When we begin to take God at His Word that He will never leave us nor forsake us (Heb. 13:5; Deut. 31:6) and that He is in control of everything, then our response to life's struggles will be different. David had blind trust in God and declared boldly in Psalm 138:7: "Though I walk in the midst of trouble, thou wilt revive me." Furthermore he states in Psalm 37:23, "The steps of a good man are ordered by the LORD." The anointing that rested on David and the anointing that God is about to pour out on this generation will cause you to sit in the midst of trouble (famine, peril, nakedness, opposition, haters, jealous folks, etc.) with a smile on your face.

The Bible declares in Psalm 66:10–19:

> For thou, O God, hast proved us: thou hast tried us, as silver is tried. Thou broughtest us into the net; thou laidst affliction upon our loins. Thou hast caused men to ride over our heads; we went through fire and through water: but thou broughtest us out into a wealthy place. I will go into thy house with burnt offerings: I will pay thee my vows, Which my lips have uttered, and my mouth hath spoken, when I was in trouble. I will offer unto thee burnt sacrifices of fatlings, with the incense of rams; I will offer bullocks with goats. Selah. Come and hear, all ye that fear God, and I will declare what he hath done for my soul. I cried unto him with my mouth, and he was extolled with my tongue. If I regard iniquity in my heart, the Lord will not hear me: But verily God hath heard me; he hath attended to the voice of my prayer.

The psalmist acknowledges that the test and afflictions are allowed by God. He goes on to say that it was God that caused men to triumph over our heads and also that it is He (God) who takes us through fire and water but at the end will bring us out and into a wealthy place. The psalmist concluded that both the trials and the wealthy place come from God. This Psalm shows clearly that the prerequisite for the wealthy place is God's mentoring fire. The psalmist goes on to say that now that he is in his wealthy place, he will pay the vows he made unto God while he was in trouble (in his process). This is a perfect example of how we are to react to trials. In other words, the aftereffect (after we would have been tried and proven) should position us to that place in which God intended, a place of strength and maturity (better and not bitter) even to the place of fulfilling His will.

The giants in the kingdom must rise up to that place in God where in spite of anything they will cover, protect, intercede, and minister to God's people, even those who were a part of their troubles. Everybody wants to experience the glory; but, again, it comes with a story (a price). During perilous times people make all sorts of promises to God, but once the memory of those trials are over those promises are soon forgotten. God will keep His end of the bargain, which is after we have suffered awhile the glory shall be revealed (Rom. 8:18), and we ought to do the same. The psalmist further says in verse eighteen, "If I regard [esteem, honor] iniquity in my heart, the Lord will not hear me" (Ps. 66:18). God's elect and chosen vessels cannot be carriers of the anointing and carry iniquity at the same time; they will have to choose one or the other.

BITTERNESS WILL SUFFOCATE YOU

The aftereffect can determine if you will operate in the anointing that you have paid the price for (was processed for). Great men and women who are being used and will be used by God will be further developed under extreme pressure. This pressure can come from anybody, even those you least expect (spouses, children, friends, parishioners, leaders, employees, or employers, etc.). If not properly managed, unreleased pressure, after its purpose of exposing what's on the inside is completed, can easily result in bitterness, anger, resentment, frustration, and so forth; this will stagnate, smother, and eventually stop the flow of God's anointing in your life. A popular phrase in the church is, I am "too blessed to be stressed." Yet on the job or at home some of these same folks can be heard saying, "God must have forgotten me." We have to speak life to seemingly dead situations. God is moved by faith, and we are told that faith comes by hearing (Rom. 10:17). If what is spoken is contradictory and defies faith, then we are doomed to fail.

The apostle Paul declares:

> Let no corrupt communication proceed out of your mouth, but that which is good to the use of edifying, that it may minister grace unto the hearers. And grieve not the Holy Spirit of God, whereby ye are sealed unto the day of redemption. Let all bitterness, and wrath, and anger, and clamour, and evil speaking, be put away from you, with all malice: And be ye kind one to another, tenderhearted, forgiving one another, even as God for Christ's sake hath forgiven you.
> —EPHESIANS 4:29–32

The apostle Paul is saying that the chosen of God must not let corrupt words come out of their mouths because they will destroy and not minister to the hearers. After God's orchestrated mentoring fire (people, circumstances, situations), it is possible to become so bitter that our very speech is sneered with curses or ill words. Some folks, though ignorant, have allowed the enemy to use their mouths as weapons to bring about much pain and grief. Common phrases such as, "You will never amount to anything," or "You are just like your no-good mother (or father)," or "You cannot…" have been tools used by Satan to play on the emotions of people to defeat them.

Moreover, the spirit of sabotage is escalating in churches to the extent that many prayer warriors have overtly refused to stand in the gap for God's people. Some of God's warriors have become so bitter because of the vicissitudes of life that they have declared that they will not speak life or blessings upon certain people that have come against them. A true man or woman of God, no matter what they have been through or even who has put them through it, will not be content until they have seen God's chosen people excel financially and spiritually, and experience the greater.

I truly believe that this is your season of revelation, elevation, and manifestation. My friend, you cannot afford to become bitter. Remember, God has called us to strengthen the weak among us even if it means that they become stronger than we are. Believing that praying for the success of others will take away from who we are is a deception created by the enemy to keep us in bondage. This is not the case at all. In fact, interceding for others enhances us and seals what is declared in Galatians 6:2: "Bear ye one another's burdens, and so fulfill the law of Christ." As we stand in the gap for God's people, God Himself will stand in the gap for us. A cold, unforgiving heart will quench the fire of God in your life.

The apostle Paul says in Ephesians 4:31 that bitterness, anger, wrath, evil speaking, etc., must be put away from us or it will grieve (hurt, mourn) the Holy Spirit of God. When we seek to destroy another, even in self-defense or unprovoked, we are still jeopardizing the anointing that lies within us. The Spirit of God will not preside in a vessel where there is bickering, lashing out, or fighting; rather these sorts of things grieve the Spirit of God. The Holy Spirit is the anointing and the anointing is the Holy Spirit. Therefore, if we hurt (grieve) the Holy Spirit, we also hurt and injure the anointing. The apostle Paul goes on to say that we must be kind one to another, not bitter but tenderhearted, forgiving one another, even as God has forgiven us for Christ's sake.

In the midst of what looks like a bad situation, we must speak of the goodness of the Lord and testify to God's ability to deliver. Moreover, we must encourage ourselves and those around us to have faith and cling to the Word of God, for it holds the promises of life. The psalmist David declared: "Before I was afflicted I went astray: but now have I kept thy word. Thou art good and doest good; teach me thy statutes" (Ps. 119:67–68). David realized that before he experienced the trials of life he was not concerned about keeping God's commandments, but after going through diverse trials and tribulations it left him with a desire to walk the plumb line; and in doing so he was able to come into the fullness of what God had in store for him.

The things that we are going through will make us better when our desire is to see the goodness of God and keep the precepts of God's law. We are able to endure hardship because we are persuaded that nothing past or present will have a terminating effect on our destiny because God, who has started us on this course, will see to it that it is completed (Phil. 1:6). David put the icing on the cake when he declared that God is good even when it seems bad (Ps. 119:68). Remember, the refiner's fire is controlled by the smith who seeks only to purify the gold; even so our lives are fashioned by God to lead us to success. All the hurts, disappointments, lack, struggles, pain, frustration, betrayal, and so forth are a part of the obstacle course that leads us to total fulfillment and to delight in the ability of our God to deliver us from all evil.

It is only when we make up our minds to ride the waves of trials and let God sail our ship that we can be propelled to our destiny. And only then can God entrust us with the greater anointing (hundredfold power). Bitterness smothers destiny but becoming better breathes destiny.

What is your aftereffect going to be: bitter against those who God used to make, mold, and shape you; or better to bring deliverance, healing, breakthrough, prosperity, and change to those same individuals who opposed you? Remember, to whom much is given, much is required (Luke 12:48).

Jesus, the greatest example of God's love toward humanity, demonstrated to us how we ought to respond to crisis. In the face of a cruel act, crucifixion, Jesus cried, "Father, forgive them; for they know not what they do" (Luke 23:34). He chose to embrace the better through forgiveness. When we allow bitterness to dwell in our hearts, it blocks forgiveness and festers resentment. Many persons are dying spiritually because of bitterness. It is so important that we are spiritually rehabilitated (restored to good spiritual health) after coming through God's mentoring process, so that we can effectively minister to God's people with unconditional love. Love is the substratum and prerequisite to operate in God's power (anointing).

Choose to Be Better Not Bitter

You might be concluding that it is much too difficult to choose the better response. I am not saying that it will be easy, but be assured that it is possible to do. Some situations will take every fiber of your being to walk away with a smile on your face and the love of God in your heart. That is why we must check into heaven's clinic to be restored. Even Jesus, after His tedious forty days and forty nights in the wilderness, had to be rehabilitated. The Bible says in Matthew 4:1 that "Jesus was led up by the Spirit into the wilderness to be tempted by the devil" (NKJV). I believe this was one of the most trying times in Jesus' life. Here He was hungry, weary, and lonely and the tempter makes a promise to fulfill all of these needs if He would worship him. As hard as this experience must have been, it was a necessary test to determine Jesus' readiness for the task that was set before Him. My friend, what you are experiencing is necessary for the task that is ahead of you.

Yes the Spirit (God's Spirit) led Jesus into the wilderness, not the devil; the devil was only being used for Jesus' schooling. Too often we give Satan credit for things that he is not entitled to. One of the most popular statements, even in the church, is, "The devil made me do it." The devil does not have that much power; some stuff, even bad things, are allowed by God to mature us and to bring us to a place of perfection. However, we know the enemy is present through our trouble just looking for a way to defeat us. But after his attacks, God always refreshes and revives us.

Jesus Himself, after going through the school of hard

knocks, was ministered to by angels and prepared to face the world. The Bible states: "Then the devil leaveth him [Jesus], and, behold, angels came and ministered unto him" (Matt. 4:11). If we stand our ground when faced with trials and refuse to give up, we will receive the reward that comes from faithful stewardship. After Jesus came out of the refiner's fire, God rehabilitated, restored, reconditioned, reconstructed, and refurbished Him. This is what God wants to do to those of us who have endured hardship.

Therefore, spiritual rehabilitation (restoration) must take place so that we can operate in the better and not the bitter. David said, "Restore unto me the joy of thy salvation; and uphold me with thy free spirit" (Ps. 51:12). David was telling the Lord he had a serious aftereffect from what he'd been through; he lost his joy; "Lord, would you please give it back to me." David goes on to say, "Then I will teach transgressors thy ways; and sinners shall be converted unto thee" (v. 13). In other words, when the joy is there he could operate in the right spirit, the anointing would flow and the kingdom of God would increase.

Rehabilitation after the fiery furnace is a must!

Rehabilitation (treatment, therapy, healing) after the fiery furnace, lion's den, shipwreck, starvation, stoning, humiliation, imprisonment, whipping, and betrayal is a difficult task; but it must take place. The word *rehabilitate* means to restore to good condition, operation, or capacity or to overhaul or to repair. After a process of hostility and nerve-wracking experiences, an individual must be rehabilitated in order to operate and function in their full capacity (innate ability).

In the U.S. Army, for instance, a soldier in intense combat can sometimes develop a mental condition called shell shock, better known today as post-traumatic stress disorder (PTSD). Soldiers who have fought on the battlefield often describe it as a combination of extreme excitement and gut-wrenching terror. Just as those military soldiers experience excitement and gut-wrenching terror while on the battlefield, so are the experiences of those called to this greater (hundredfold) anointing. The excitement is found in operating in the miraculous and watching God move by His Spirit to touch frail humanity as God exalts us with manifold blessings. On the other hand there is a gut-wrenching within us as the vicious lies, attacks, betrayals, mistreatments, oppositions, haters, and enemies try to annihilate us in an attempt to frustrate our purpose in life.

Intense combat can also do such damage to the emotions that it can even cause permanent health damage. Those who have been called to walk in the power and glory of God, after paying the price (great suffering and intense warfare), must not come out emotionally scarred and physically challenged. The danger of this is that it prevents you from operating in the fullness of the anointing and from carrying out God's assignment. Post-traumatic stress disorder (PTSD) has also been known as battle fatigue. After and during God's orchestrated mentoring fire, you (God's militant soldier) can easily develop this condition (I call it the giving up or the no more fight syndrome). This can hamper the entire plan and purpose of God for your kingdom assignment. You must fight when you don't feel like fighting, push even when you don't feel like pushing, and watch God play you like an instrument. Do not allow battle fatigue to overtake you. Develop the attitude of the apostle Paul and "press toward [not away from] the mark for the prize [greater anointing] of the high calling of God in Christ Jesus" (Phil. 3:14).

Post-traumatic stress disorder (PTSD), or shell shock, is

characterized by symptoms such as memory loss, altered mood, trouble concentrating, disturbed sleeping patterns, nightmares, flashbacks, fatigue, muscle and joint pains, headaches, skin conditions, irritability, outbursts of anger, and episodes of anxiety and panic. In the natural these illnesses and conditions could disqualify the soldiers from ever fighting in battle again. They were sent off the battlefield and in times past were even shot to death for cowardice. In other words, to the military they were useless because of their conditions.

Similarly, when those called of God who have been processed by His mentoring fire and come out bitter and not better, they are automatically dismissed from their task. The work of God will continue with or without us. We can be sure that God will raise someone up to do His work. When the Jews (His chosen people) rejected Him (God), He went and found Himself a people that did not know Him, the Gentiles, and used them for His glory. God wants faithful people who will work while it is day; those who will understand that the process is to shape their character so that they will carry out their assignment in God's kingdom in the spirit of excellence.

When we, as soldiers of God's army, allow bitterness, hatred, anger, resentment, or frustration to take us over because of the hostility of the battlefield, vicious attacks from our opponents, dry seasons, disappointment, betrayal, verbal abuse, and much more, we then become useless to the body of Christ (God's army). Moreover, in this state you can become hazardous to the flock of God; hence discharge is necessary.

Soldiers that develop post-traumatic stress disorder (PTSD) experience symptoms as stated earlier such as flashbacks. A flashback is a recurring, intensely vivid image of a past traumatic experience. In other words, their past experience of hostility and danger would flash back in their mental capacity as a movie being replayed, causing them to remember their bad experiences in combat and with their enemies. These memories can result in unusual outburst of anger and revenge, putting the soldier in the defensive mode where he might attack someone, possibly even his own comrades.

Wow! Does that sound familiar to you? Someone who you know for certain is anointed by God but stays on the defensive and causes injury in the kingdom rather than building it? That's why we must be rehabilitated in order to effectively operate in the anointing. We need a divine encounter with God.

ANOINTED TO REPRESENT THE KING OF KINGS

The men and women of God who will be entrusted with this power-packed hundredfold anointing at the end of their process, must come out of it better and not bitter. The servants of God in this season will be carrying too much power (anointing, spiritual artillery) to be having flashbacks of what they have been through and what people have done to them; therefore, they must be rehabilitated. Can you imagine a man or woman of God in a powerful deliverance service under an unusual anointing speaking into the lives of God's people suddenly being given a word of deliverance and change by God for a particular individual in the congregation? And after calling out that individual suddenly remembering (flashback) that this is one of the persons that came up against them causing them great anguish and pain. My friend, without rehabilitation the word for that individual will not be words of deliverance or change but words of doom. This is not the ideal state to be in because it renders you ineffective for ministry and God is forced to dismiss you from service. The true vessels of God must be able to maintain professionalism and integrity regardless of previous encounters.

What is your decision, to come out bitter or better? The only flashback we should have is that of the psalmist David. King David declares in Psalm 105:5: "Remember his marvelous works that he hath done; his wonders, and the judgments of his mouth."

Whatever God allows you to experience will, at the end of the day, be marvelous (fantastic, phenomenal, stupendous). Yes, even what He allows people to do to you will bring great joy to your life. Let me be a little more specific: church folks, spouses, family, friends, and associates will at the end of the day cause you to become incredible. Wow! You should be shouting now! Why? As Joseph said to his brothers, we can also declare: They meant it for evil but God meant it for the incredible (so extraordinary as to seem impossible)!

Chapter Six

GREATER WORKS

WE ARE IN a season where God is eager to manifest His power through persons who are willing and available. As Jesus said in John 14:12, "He who believes in Me...greater works than these shall he do" (NKJV). While this might seem strange to many, this is not new to the prophets of old who were willing to pay the price for the greater anointing. People like Peter knew what it meant to operate in the "greater" as he walked past the sick and his shadow cast a healing balm. Paul's "greater" was expressed in terms of his vigor to spread the gospel to a nation that did not know his God; he cast out demons, had people healed by a handkerchief or apron taken from him, and much more. God wants to take a people to a place that no man has gone before. The greater anointing will be manifested in the lives of those who have been called and processed. Are you willing to pay the price?

There are a variety of ways that "greater works" has been interpreted over the years. However, for this particular chapter we will be referring to "greater works" as something spiritual (word or deed) that is naturally astounding or mind-blowing. I refer to the definition supplied by Webster's dictionary to express the underlying meaning of "greater works" as follows: The word *greater* is defined as "unusual or incomprehensible in degree, power and intensity; an extreme or notable degree." *Work* is defined as "exertion or effort directed to produce or accomplish something, productive or operative activity, to act or operate effectively."

The time has come for the true warriors to come forth, those who are willing to redefine the "greater" in terms of spiritual explosion as opposed to lavish cathedrals, priestly garments, and words that tickle the ear. We are living in the finest hours of the church, the time in which God will reveal the mysteries (hidden secrets) of His kingdom to this entire world. We who are His disciples will do greater works than the works that Jesus did while He was here on earth. There is no reason why the dead cannot be raised, the sick healed, sinners come to repentance, and people delivered from all manner of strongholds.

These works are possible to all believers; but remember, God will only do this through His chosen vessels those who have been tested, tried, and proven. It is time for the greater works. Aren't you tired of church as usual? I don't know about you, but I am ready to see the multitude come to Jesus Christ. I am ready to see the blind eyes opened, the lame walk, the deaf hear, the dumb talk, the sick healed, and the dead raised. My friends, this is the hour in which God will pour out His Spirit upon all flesh as He declared through His servant Joel (Joel 2:28).

Harnessing the Greater

If you have been processed through God's orchestrated mentoring fire, get ready for a spiritual explosion that has never been seen before: greater works. Jesus said:

Verily, verily, I say unto you, He that believeth on me,
the works that I do shall he do also; and greater works
than these shall he do; because I go unto my Father.

—JOHN 14:12

If you have been processed through God's orchestrated mentoring fire, get ready for a spiritual explosion.

Jesus was telling Philip that the supernatural working power and anointing of God (the Holy Spirit) was not limited to Him alone but that God was preparing them to harness this power-packed anointing as well and that it would come upon them after Jesus' ascension. And not only would they do the works that He (Jesus) did but even greater works. Jesus will ensure that we receive just what is needed for our assignment.

Like in the natural, a promotion in the spiritual realm comes with a price, tangible or intangible. For instance, the reason you might be experiencing a heavy season of warfare and fierce battles is because you have been handpicked by God to operate in this final outpouring of His anointing and power upon the earth. The enemy knows that God has destined you to be among those who will usher in the great ingathering and to spread the message of salvation through supernatural demonstrations of word, deed, and action.

The cry of many servants of God is that there is too much persecution and too many attacks. However, we know that God is moving among us; when the enemy is fighting strong, we must endure, for the greater will come forth in due time.

> When the enemy is fighting strong, we must
> endure, for the greater will come forth in due time.

The servants of God will pay to operate in this anointing but the following must be considered. Firstly, the vessel (you) must be prepared to harness the anointing that God has predetermined for your life. Secondly, you have to be willing to pay the price; the only way to be prepared to carry such great power and anointing is to experience trials and tribulations in abundance—in other words, great, great suffering. Remember, after you have suffered awhile the glory shall be revealed. My comrade, you are not brass or silver but pure gold, and after the fire God will take you higher and beyond that which can be conceived.

Doing greater works than Jesus is not a license for selfishness and personal gain (see Simon the sorcerer in Acts 8). This awesome gift is not to fester pride or make the saints arrogant but so that the gospel of Jesus Christ can be made more relevant in the lives of today's generation. Our children, for instance, are watching movies that glorify witches and other satanic personalities, wearing clothing dedicated to witches, and playing Ouija boards and other dark age games while the Christians are home singing "Satan's under my feet." As anointed people of God, we must get radical and take back what the devil has stolen from us.

Here's what Jesus said in Matthew 11:12: "And from the days of John the Baptist until now the kingdom of heaven suffereth violence, and the violent take it by force." God wants some trained and tested warriors who will leap over walls and run through troops in these final days.

OPERATING IN AUTHORITY

We must take back what the enemy has stolen from us. This taking back from the enemy requires us to go beyond the norm. Therefore, as the body of Christ, we must exercise our spiritual gifting and authority. It was this sort of exercise that allowed the godly leaders of yesteryears to be such great witnesses. David slew Goliath the giant with a sling and a stone, and the Philistines knew that his God was God. Daniel was thrown into a den full of hungry lions and came out unharmed, and those who witnessed this confessed that his God is Lord. Esther risked her life to go before the king to plead the case of the Jews, and in the end the decree was established to honor her God. The list goes on of persons who walked in the greater; for each the result was a revival or great awakening to the fact that God Almighty reigns. The supernatural is calling for the remnant.

Remember what the great apostle Paul said in 2 Corinthians 4:17: "Our light affliction, which is but for a moment, worketh for us a far more exceeding and eternal weight of glory." The affliction is light but the glory (the anointing) that shall come upon you will be weighty, heavy. Do not let the afflictions detour you; because at the end of the day when you see what God has set aside for you, you will forget the process because of the magnitude of the promise. You are God's chosen vessel! My friends, after you have experienced such great trials and tribulations, the after-effect (whether you become bitter or better) will determine whether you are qualified by God to be entrusted with such uncommon, unusual hundredfold power and anointing for the greater works of the kingdom. After passing all tests and fulfilling all the requirements, you will then be declared a kingdom specialist, one who is capable of carrying out any task for the Master. Are you willing to pay?

MOVING FROM THE LESSER TO THE GREATER ANOINTING

Greater works are not limited to miracles, signs, and wonders. There are several elements that are necessary to move into the greater. Firstly, a prayer-filled life is the most essential requirement for operating in the greater. A famous slogan among the Christian arena is "no prayer no power!" Prayer is vital. It allows us to communicate with God and for God to speak to us. If we are not constantly in prayer, then we cannot be aware of the will of God. It is no wonder that some churches are operating as businesses rather than spiritual institutes. When God is kept as our primary advisor and/or director, then we make ourselves available to what God wants to do in and through us. Moreover, we can be led by Jesus' example of doing ministry; while He was on earth He took time out to pray. The Gospel writers have Jesus taking a boat to a serene place to pray (Mark 1:31), praying before meals (Matt. 14:19), even praying at the grave of Lazarus (John 11:41–42), and prior to His crucifixion Jesus is in Gethsemane praying on three occasions while the disciples slept (Matt. 26:36, 39, 42). The necessity of prayer cannot be stressed enough, yet in our churches prayer meetings are the least supported events. In private settings, a pastor's personal life, prayer often takes second place to church programs. Prayer is the key to unfolding the greater anointing in our lives.

Secondly, to operate in the greater we must be willing to keep God's commandments. Too many people, including ministers, are walking in disobedience to God's laws and are not living up to His standard of holiness. God is looking for vessels that He can trust with the greater, persons who are sold out to living lives that are pleasing to God. It has become common for people to believe that God's mandate for holy living has been adjusted to fit the pleasures and evil desires of humanity. God's law still stands:

> For I am the Lord your God: ye shall therefore sanctify yourselves, and ye shall be holy; for I am holy.
> —Leviticus 11:44

The greater is described as a supernatural undertaking and hence suggests a spiritual undercurrent of power. It is believed that when Jesus said that He will send us a Comforter who would guide us into all truth (John 16:7–13) that He knew that we needed to be undergirded by a higher power (the Spirit of God). God's Spirit is the enabler of the saints to carry out the ministry that God has entrusted to His children. As is noted in Scripture, this fight is "not against flesh and blood" but rather we are in the midst of spiritual warfare and we are fighting "against principalities, against powers, against the rulers of the darkness of this world, against spiritual wickedness in high places" (Eph. 6:12). We are failing miserably because we are using the wrong tools in this battle. We cannot fight spirit with flesh; we must fight spirit with Spirit. It is through the Spirit of the living God that we will defeat our adversaries.

> Not by might, nor by power, but by my Spirit, saith the Lord of hosts.
> —Zechariah 4:6

In this season of the greater we must be filled (by the Spirit) in order to fulfill His will.

You are destined for greatness. Are you willing to pay the price?

NOTES

CHAPTER THREE

1. Theodore Rubin quote found at http://thinkexist.com/quotation/the_problem_is_not_that_there_are_problems-the/8372.html (accessed January 31, 2013).

2. Jean Paul Richter quote found at http://thinkexist.com/quotation/sleep-riches-and_health-to_be_truly_enjoyed-must/169079.html (accessed January 31, 2013).

3. Mike Murdock, *The Assignment: The Pain & The Passion, Volume 4* (Fort Worth, TX: Wisdom International, 1999).

4. Myles Munroe, *The Glory of Living* (Shippensburg, PA: Destiny Image, 2005), 113.

5. African proverb found at http://quonation.com/quote/14403 (accessed January 31, 2013).

CHAPTER FOUR

1. Lori Wilke, *The Costly Anointing* (Shippensburg, PA: Destiny Image, 2001), 62.

2. Ervin N. Hershberger, *Seeing Christ in the Tabernacle* (Harrisburg, PA: Vision Publishers, 2007).

CHAPTER FIVE

1. Edmond Burke quote found at http://www.netawd.com/q/?id=1181 (accessed February 1, 2013).

ABOUT THE AUTHOR

Apostle Reno I. Johnson is the founding Pastor of Divine Encounter Ministries International, which was established on December 6, 2009, the place where Divinity transforms humanity.

He is a highly sought after anointed messenger of God, he is a Warrior of the faith, an excellent Teacher of God's Word and a Dynamic, Radical Preacher, whose passion is to heal the hurting, usher souls into the Kingdom of God and destroy the works of the devil. Prior to entering the ministry, Apostle Johnson was employed as a certified electronic technician; he obtained an Associate's Degree in Electronics from the New England Institute of Technology in West Palm Beach, Florida. However, upon receiving the call to ministry, Apostle Johnson pursued several biblical degrees including courses at the Principles of Life Bible College (Nassau, Bahamas); a Diploma in Biblical Studies at Liberty University (Lynchburg, Virginia), and an Associate's Degree at the Cornerstone Christian University (Orlando, Florida).

At present Apostle Johnson is pursuing a higher level of Biblical Studies at the Cornerstone Christian University (Orlando, Florida). He was consecrated to the office of an Apostle on December 5, 2010.

He currently resides in Nassau, Bahamas, with his wife, Lady Shandaly Johnson and their two daughters, Ranaé and Reishonda.

Apostle Johnson's primary focus is to set the captives free, equip the Body of Christ, and expand the kingdom of God.

CONTACT THE AUTHOR

E-mail:

arjgodsgeneral@aol.com

Websites:

www.ARJM.org

www.DEMISITE.org

MINISTRY RESOURCES

CD List

Sermon Title	Order #
Following God to a Dead End	ARJ029
You won't Frustrate my Purpose	ARJ073
Preserved for a Purpose	ARJ075
Preparation of the Promise	ARJ079
The Promises of God	ARJ083
It's a matter of Life or Death	ARJ086
The Anointing	ARJ087
I am Desperate	ARJ089
The Promise	ARJ090
The Just shall live by Faith	ARJ091
It's time to move forward	ARJ092
The secret Place	ARJ093
The Providence of God	ARJ094
The Season of Wonders	ARJ095
Be Still	AJR096
'Don't Stop Digging'	ARJ097
'Trusting in God'	ARJ098

DVD List

Sermon Title	Order #
It's time to move	ARJD077
God gat me covered	ARJD078
Preparation for the Promise	ARJD079
It's my Time now	ARJD080
The Birth of the Apostolic Church	ARJD081
Marked for Greatness	ARJD082
The Promises of God	ARJD083
I am more than a Conqueror	ARJD085
It's a matter of Life or Death	ARJD086
The Anointing	ARJD087
An Abundance of Rain	ARJD088
I Am Desperate	ARJD089
The Promise	ARJD090
The Just shall live by Faith	ARJD091
It's time to move forward	ARJD092
The Secret Place	ARJD093
The Providence of God	ARJD094
The Season of Wonders	ARJD095
Be Still	ARJD096
Don't Stop Digging	ARJD097
Trusting in God	ARJD098

CDs: $8.00 (plus $3.95 shipping and handling)

DVDs: $12.00 (plus $3.95 shipping and handling)

Make all checks payable to Divine Favour Ltd.

To order Apostle Reno I. Johnson's Ministry Resources you can call or write to:

Mailing Address

Apostle Reno I. Johnson Ministries Int'l
US: P.O. Box 6680 Lake Worth, FL. 33466
Tel.: 561-370-7667* 203-514-9318 (U.K)

Or

BH: P.O. Box GT-2819* Nassau, Bahamas.
Tel.: 242-341-4700/5700* 225-7222

ALSO BY APOSTLE RENO I. JOHNSON:

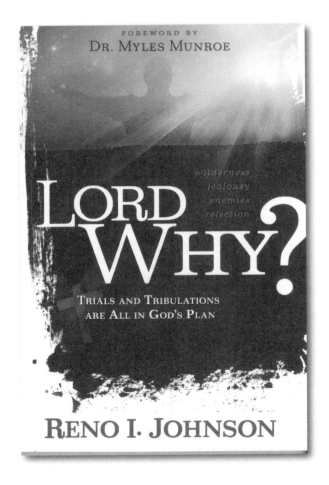

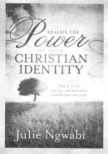

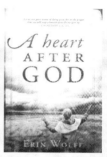